KATE'S DAUGHTER

THE REAL CATHERINE COOKSON

Books by Catherine Cookson

NOVELS

Kate Hannigan
The Fifteen Streets
Colour Blind
Maggie Rowan
Rooney
The Menagerie
Slinky Jane
Fanny McBride
Fenwick Houses
Heritage of Folly
The Garment
The Fen Tiger
The Blind Miller
House of Men
Hannah Massey
The Long Corridor
The Unbaited Trap
Katie Mulholland
The Round Tower
The Nice Bloke
The Glass Virgin
The Invitation
The Dwelling Place
Feathers in the Fire
Pure as the Lily
The Mallen Streak
The Mallen Girl
The Mallen Litter
The Invisible Cord
The Gambling Man
The Tide of Life
The Slow Awakening
The Iron Façade
The Girl
The Cinder Path
Miss Martha Mary Crawford
The Man Who Cried
Tilly Trotter
Tilly Trotter Wed
Tilly Trotter Widowed

The Whip
Hamilton
The Black Velvet Gown
Goodbye Hamilton
A Dinner of Herbs
Harold
The Moth
Bill Bailey
The Parson's Daughter
Bill Bailey's Lot
The Cultured Handmaiden
Bill Bailey's Daughter
The Harrogate Secret
The Black Candle
The Wingless Bird
The Gillyvors
My Beloved Son
The Rag Nymph
The House of Women
The Maltese Angel
The Year of the Virgins
The Golden Straw
Justice is a Woman
The Tinker's Girl
A Ruthless Need
The Obsession
The Upstart
The Branded Man
The Bonny Dawn
The Bondage of Love
The Desert Crop
The Lady on My Left
The Solace of Sin
Riley
The Blind Years
The Thursday Friend
A House Divided
Kate Hannigan's Girl
Rosie of the River
The Silent Lady

THE MARY ANN STORIES
A Grand Man
Life and Mary Ann
The Lord and Mary Ann
Marriage and Mary Ann
The Devil and Mary Ann
Mary Ann's Angels
Love and Mary Ann
Mary Ann and Bill

FOR CHILDREN
Matty Doolin
Mrs Flannagan's Trumpet
Joe and the Gladiator
Go Tell It To Mrs Golightly
The Nipper
Lanky Jones
Rory's Fortune
Nancy Nutall and the Mongrel
Our John Willie
Bill and the Mary Ann Shaughnessy

AUTOBIOGRAPHY
Our Kate
Let Me Make Myself Plain
Catherine Cookson Country
Plainer Still
Just a Saying

SHORT STORIES
The Simple Soul and other Stories

POETRY
Just A Saying

KATE'S DAUGHTER
THE REAL
CATHERINE COOKSON

PIERS DUDGEON

BANTAM PRESS

LONDON · NEW YORK · TORONTO · SYDNEY · AUCKLAND

TRANSWORLD PUBLISHERS
61-63 Uxbridge Road, London W5 5SA
a division of The Random House Group Ltd

RANDOM HOUSE AUSTRALIA (PTY) LTD
20 Alfred Street, Milsons Point, Sydney,
New South Wales 2061, Australia

RANDOM HOUSE NEW ZEALAND LTD
18 Poland Road, Glenfield, Auckland 10, New Zealand

RANDOM HOUSE SOUTH AFRICA (PTY) LTD
Endulini, 5a Jubilee Road, Parktown 2193, South Africa

Published 2003 by Bantam Press
a division of Transworld Publishers

A catalogue record for this book is available
from the British Library.
ISBN 0593 051416

Written, designed and produced by Piers Dudgeon
Printed by Tien Wah Press (PTE.) Limited, Singapore

1 3 5 7 9 10 8 6 4 2

Papers used by Transworld Publishers are natural, recyclable products
made from wood grown in sustainable forests. The manufacturing processes conform to the
environmental regulations of the country of origin.

CONTENTS

By Jarrow's Lake   6

On Stony Ground   9

Unwanted Seed   18

White Light   44

Up By The Roots   53

Break Out   75

Breakdown   93

Happy Families   133

A Beggar on Horseback   142

Becoming Kate   179

Acknowledgments   192

1 By Jarrow's Lake

If, on August 4, 1832, you had chanced to walk down the Jarrow Road on the south bank of the Tyne towards South Shields, your eyes would have met an unsettling sight. A gibbet had been erected on the oily black mudflats known as Jarrow Slake. On it was hung a curved metal cage, iron bars welded together to hold the corpse of a local pitman, William Jobling, who had been hanged the day before for murder, even though his supposed victim, a magistrate by name of Nicholas Fairles, had exonerated him before he died. Jobling's real crime was to walk out on strike in protest over 'bonding', an employer practice one step away from slave labour. As a warning to others, his body was put under military guard and left to putrefy for more than three weeks. The penalty for removing it was death. When, finally, the guard disbanded, Jobling's remains disappeared over night, taken down by the poor man's family.

There are many stories attached to Jarrow Slake (a lazy diminutive of 'Jarrow's Lake'), some as old as Roman times, some within living memory. They are always about death or destruction.

In 1913, some eighty years after Jobling was hanged, Reny Harding was born just opposite the Slake, at No. 17 William Black Street, and remembers the pond's use as a tidal timber store. Great lengths of unsawn timber were lashed together into an enormous raft, secured to upright posts, awaiting the attentions of the nearby saw mill. 'There was wood all across the water,' she remembers, 'right up to the gut wall. We would walk across it, and there was a hut in the middle, where Granda Tulip was

Katie would boast to her companions about her skill in playing the piano on the Slake or Slacks, jumping from timber to timber. Below, the effigy of William Jobling.

the caretaker. He looked after the Slacks, but he never chased us off. My father had his own boat, he called it Irene, and at one time he used to take all the children up river to see the big boats, the Venus, the Queen Elizabeth. Anyway, me father was taking a lot out and Matthew McHaffie missed the boat so he got a sculler boat from some people called Lamb and went after me father's boat and the river swelled up just as he was passing this wall and the swell caught him and he drowned. It's something to do with the tide. Me father blamed himself for that.'

Winnie Richardson, the daughter of a miner, born three years earlier than Reny in Philipson Street, which ran back-to-back with William Black Street, remembers that the timber pond was not itself dangerous, but the gut – outflow of the River Don – was both deep and fast, and at ebb tide could be perilous indeed. Matthew McHaffie was not the only person to be caught up in it. Winnie and Reny's neighbour, a raven-haired Irish girl called Catherine McMullen and known as Katie, once pushed a boy called Billy into the Slake and held his head down under the scum and driftwood and vegetable refuse. If it hadn't been for a man seeing what she was doing from the top deck of a tram, waiting nearby at the crossing opposite the old chemical works, 'wor Billy', as the victim's irate father later referred to him, might not have survived.

Forty years later the same Katie McMullen wrote a book called *The Fifteen Streets*, in which a girl with her name was swept away to her death in

Producer Ray Marshall's faithful TV film of The Fifteen Streets *showed Katie and her friend Christine in their boat, their arms wound tightly round one another at the end, sucked into the currents of the Gut, to disappear beneath the oozing morass of the Slake, while Katie's brother, John, from the nearby staithes, tried desperately to save them.*

a boat on the gut, a heart-rending tale of destruction which put Katie centre stage as a sweet child wronged by fate, fulfilling her tragic destiny in the murky depths of the Slake – not at all how Billy had seen it the day he nearly drowned.

Katie McMullen never could get over the Slake as a place of destruction. Like the pool in which Narcissus fell in love with his own reflection, it became a symbolic mirror to a destructive instinct from whose power she could not break free. She returned to it in the nightmare of breakdown, and in the novel, *Katie Mulholland*, her heroine returns to the horror of it daily.

As so often in her books, the fiction does not so much reflect the facts as illuminate Catherine's true-life feelings, which lie behind them.

2 ON STONY GROUND

The map, published in 1897, shows the first completed houses on Simonside Terrace and William Black Street, south of Jarrow Slake. St Paul's Monastery, where Bede lived and worked, is to the north west; Tyne Dock to the east.

Katie's country, East Jarrow, was quite distinct from the town of Jarrow to the west, it comprised three streets and two terraces set in wasteland surrounded by fields across the Jarrow Road from the Slake. 'It was like a little island on its own,' remembers Reny. There were no other houses for a quarter of a mile or so.

The estate had been constructed by the Larkins, proprietors of the St Bede Chemical Works, who traded on the Slake's western flank from the late 19th century. It was built in the shape of an E, the two terraces called Simonside making up the long member and looking north across the river, the three shorter members dropping down from them Lancaster Street, and, back-to-back Philipson Street and at the east end, William Black Street.

First, the Larkins built a couple of mansions for themselves in Simonside Terrace, with a drive up to the house – 'lovely self-contained houses,' as Reny recalls, 'it was the posh part.' Then came the houses in William Black Street – actually the first street to be completed, as is shown in the map above of 1897. These houses were divided into what we would call maisonettes, though each apartment was referred to as a house. Reny lived at No. 17: 'My family were three brothers and a sister, and then me. Florrie was seven years older, same age as Katie McMullen. My oldest brother was one year older, then ten and eight – our Bill, Jim, then Jack. My father was a trimmer on the railways at Tyne Dock. We thought ourselves fortunate because he was never out of work.'

A few doors up the street, in what was at the time a very modern, three-room, ground floor 'house' at No. 10, lived the McMullens: Grandma Rose, Stepgrandpa John, their son, Jack (who worked with John in the docks as an unskilled labourer), Katie and her unmarried

mother, also named Catherine, but known as Kate.

There was in fact quite an extended family presence, for Grandma Rose's sister, Maggie, also lived in William Black Street, as did Kate's sister, Mary, with her husband, Alec Charlton, and children Jack, Alec and Theresa (known as Teri).

The houses were well built. There was pride in living in the New Buildings, as they were called. 'The steps were always scrubbed, they were lilywhite literally,' Reny remembers, and flags not only to respectability: 'One time, during an election a woman painted her step green for the Liberal Party!'

Respectability was all, however, and the pressure to attain it caused not a little insecurity in some quarters. Aunt Mary measured her success in terms of some fine furniture, including a mahogany dining table, so treasured that she knitted four matching leggings to protect it against idle scuffs and scrapes.

There was no crime to speak of; the local bobby saw to that: 'I can remember PC Mortenson who used to live in Simonside Terrace,' Reny continued. 'He would sit in his window on his day off; you had to behave yourself; he was very strict, but very good; you know, just clip you over the ears with his gloves.'

Winnie Richardson, who lived across the back lane in Philipson Street and was three years closer to Katie in age, recalled the freedom the children enjoyed: 'There was nothing to stop you playing out. The houses were in the middle of cornfields and gardens. Mr Eckford used to till the gardens on one side and Mr Affleck was the farmer on the other side of the village. The

East Jarrow was quite distinct from Jarrow Town (pictured above). Set apart from the industrial sprawl, it sat amidst cornfields and allotments and all the children enjoyed freedom to roam. Katie's granda kept as many as 60 hens in his crees, and on a field beyond Philipson Street, she would sit on a high bank and watch the men set the rabbits off and then the dogs – often stimulated with spirits – after them. 'I have know myself cry when the rabbits were caught,' she later wrote.

Far right: John and Rose McMullen with their one child, Jack. The photograph was taken around the time of Katie's birth in 1906.

Afflecks lived in Redwood Cottage opposite the saw mill [on the south-east corner of the Slake]. There was May, Cissie and Maud, three sisters. Mr Eckford ran the little shop in Philipson Street.'

'James Eckford had three gardens on the front field, allotments,' continued Reny. 'One was a vegetable garden, so we had all fresh vegetables in the shop and the other was just a general... I'm not sure what that was for. The Eckfords lived in Simonside Terrace, and you know I told you about Granda Tulip, he lived in Simonside Terrace too, and his daughter they called Lily! – Lily Tulip, the flowergirl! She married a cousin of the Queen and they called her Lady Elphinstone, she became a Lady-in-Waiting.

'Oh, and I remember the Flannagans, two sons, Jerry and John and one of them married an ice cream girl. She was a very quiet person. Then Olive Swinburn, she was about the same age as our Florrie, Beatrice Swinburn was my friend, about my age. They were a nice family, they went to live in South Shields. They called Mr Swinburn, Sep – *Seppie Swinburn* went to live in *Seventeen Salmon Street, South Shields* – see, half of me brain IS working, my goodness!'

Below right, the New Buildings allotments – Mr Eckford, who ran the Philipson Street shop, worked them. In the opening pages of Pure As The Lily, *Catherine shows just what they meant to a working man in the 1920s.*

Reny screamed with laughter at the alliteration, but I was busy noting names she was spilling that I knew from the novels or *Our Kate*. Sep is the fellow in *The Tide of Life*, and in her teens Katie used to clean for the Flannagan family. In *The Grand Man*, Sarah Flannagan shows up Mary Ann Shaughnessy for being a liar (as, in reality, she had shown up Katie). Olive Swinburn is the girl in *Our Kate* who flattens Katie when she challenges her to a fight. Florrie Harding, who was for a period a friend of Katie, figures in a significant 'moment' in *Our Kate* when Katie watches her walk past her window with Joan Woodcock and realises that her childhood is behind her and that henceforth she will forget the children in the New Buildings and make something of her life. I asked Reny whether she remembered Joan.

'Joan Woodcock? She married our Jim! She became my sister-in-law!' she laughed. 'I can remember

when they were in their teens and were getting perhaps too keen, she was sent to her grandparents for a while.'

'There were all kinds of people in that village,' Winnie sighed, 'just the four streets, but it was such a stable community, you know. We were there a very long time and we had the same neighbours for a long time.'

Reny did the same: 'We lived there, me father died there, me son was 7 when we left. I got married there… I lived there till the late 1940s…'

Winnie, being bright at school, had trained as a teacher in Sunderland (10 miles away), and then returned as a teacher to her old school (which had been Katie's too) – St Peter & Paul's, Tyne Dock. She taught there all her working life.

Today, Winnie still lives close by. Reny married within the New Buildings, moving with her husband to Philipson Street, just one street away. She, too, lives but a walk away today. The girls' whole outlook remained narrow. Katie McMullen was in that sense very different from them. The world would become her oyster. Was that unique, or were there others who broke free or stood apart from the community?

'There was a university teacher in the Larkins' house on Simonside, well it was a mansion really,' Winnie recalled. 'The Douglases, the son rose to be in charge of Sunderland finances. He was an only child. He went on to Further Education like I did, but I don't remember anyone else did that. There were some quite

Catherine with her much loved grandma, Rose McMullen

well off. The people next door to us, the man worked at the saw mill and only had one child, they had wall-to-wall carpeting – in those days! Next door to that the man was manager of the Jarrow butcher's shop in Hope Street, and when he retired he bought a *bungalow* in Monkton! There was a big difference among the people, for there were very poor people as well, but it wasn't a slum at all.'

'There were no slums in East Jarrow,' agreed Reny with pride, before adding under her breath, 'There was only one slum, theirs, the McMullens, it was always full of beer bottles. There weren't any really well off either, but East Jarrow was one of those places where everybody helped everybody else – everybody except the McMullens.

'In the slump [the Depression of the 1920s and '30s], it was a difficult time. I remember there were miners out of work and me father bought one of them a little trap and fetched the wood into his own yard and chopped it up into sticks, just so's this miner could get a bit of work selling bundles of sticks. We were all friendly except the McMullens and I was terrified of that old man, John McMullen... Oooh!' Reny screamed. 'He was a great, big, horrible Irishman, always very loud. He would thunder at people.'

On the question of 'that old man,' Katie's step-grandfather, almost every-one was in agreement. Even McMullen's wife, Rose, would refer to him as 'a pig of a man', and his step-daughters – Sarah Lavelle (the eldest), Kate (the middle one) and Mary Charlton (the youngest) – detested him. According to Sarah's youngest daughter, also called Sarah (I'll refer to her as Cousin Sarah), 'He was why they got away from home as soon as they could.' Kate returned only when she became pregnant out of wedlock, and left again, soon after the birth, to live out in service and earn the child's keep.

I already had the story that after Aunt Sarah stayed out one night as a young woman – she'd been visiting a friend in Newcastle – John McMullen took his belt to her in the yard. Now I discovered that he had also whipped Kate, when, aged 23, she came home and announced that she was pregnant. McMullen took a razor strap to her, and almost killed her.

Katie alone, who bore his name but was of course

Below, Sarah at the time that John McMullen flayed her alive. It was a male-dominated, physical world: 'I don't think we expected men to be that friendly,' recalls Winnie.

unrelated to him, had time for John McMullen. She would call him, '*Me* da,' and later, '*Me* granda,' as opposed to 'My Aunt Sarah' or 'My Aunt Mary,' always reserving the colloquial form for those whom she really held dear, which was only ever John and Rose.

Her relations still find it difficult to understand why she always held a candle to the old man. The answer is surely that for the first six years of her life John was effectively Katie's father. However much a hard man he was to others, he never raised a hand to Katie, and her mother never dared hit her when he was in the house. Likewise, Rose gave Katie unconditional love for the six years that she was her surrogate mother, which was why, when Catherine returned to the site of William Black Street sixty years later, it was to her grandma, Rose, that her first thoughts turned, not to her real mother, Kate. Similarly, her 'connection' to John McMullen was always there, even unto the end.

I asked Winnie for a description of him: 'He was tall and he was gaunt and when I knew him, he was old. I didn't know him as a young man. He used to keep hens in his backyard, and he'd bring them up to the top where there was free land and gravel and grass and bits of stuff because of the building rubbish lying around. I used to see him but I never had anything to say to him. In those days I don't think we expected men to be that friendly, you know. I think he would be quite physical, but he did love Katie and he did bring her up, and although he was a rather hard man he begrudged her nothing.'

John McMullen was in his early fifties when Katie was born, and they enjoyed special moments together. He would share his boiled egg with her when he came home for his tea from shovelling iron ore off the boats at Tyne Dock. He would tell her stories of 'the old country' (Ireland), he would encourage her natural gift of story-telling, and she in turn would enjoy his total disrespect for the more precious people of the New Buildings who couldn't see farther than their own noses, and some of whom, as will fall clear, thought no better of Katie than of him.

Katie and John McMullen had this in common, they easily alienated people. In McMullen's case it was rooted in his birth – he was of Irish descent at a time when the Irish were largely despised for their poverty and fecklessness – and in his Irish culture: he had an

irrational hatred of Protestants, for example. In the New Buildings he was in a minority – only four other families, the Richardsons, the McArthurs, the Flannagans and the Charltons were Roman Catholic.

Right from the start, Catherine was an outsider, too. From the age of four she had attended Simonside School, which drew most of its custom not from East Jarrow but from Cleveland Place, a small, run-down community situated half a mile away from the New Buildings at the south west corner of the estate, on the south side of the main Newcastle-South Shields railway line. It was set in the midst of land known as Rooney's farm, source probably of the dustman's name in Catherine's early novel called *Rooney*.

What this meant was that when she arrived at 10 William Black Street in July 1912, few of the New Buildings children would have been known to her even through school. Most of them, if they were Protestant like Reny and the rest of the Harding children, went to East Jarrow school on Straker Terrace, just past the boundary line into Jarrow, and then to Stanhope Road School in Shields. The Catholics, like Winnie, went to St Bede's, Jarrow, and later St Peter & Paul's, Tyne Dock. Very likely in an effort to integrate Katie, she was

Women gossiping at their back doors would disperse when they saw John McMullen coming.

moved from Simonside School to East Jarrow School early in 1913, the Protestant option being taken despite the family's Catholic roots, possibly because of Katie's initial friendship with Florrie Harding.

Also, as has already been noted in respect of John McMullen, Catherine and the children of the other few Catholic families, Winnie Richardson among them, were in a minority. Winnie was a Catholic and liked Catherine – 'Katie made a fuss of me, she was a kind person. I was a little girl and I thought she was lovely, full of talk and laughter, you know?' Reny, on the other hand, was a Protestant and clearly loathed her. Winnie insisted, 'All the children played together, we were Catholics and in a bit of a minority, but I never found any difficulty, except that we didn't go to the same school, which was rather a pity.'

Nevertheless, religion represented a cultural and social division more marked than it is in England today, and was made more vivid in a close set-up like the New Buildings. Doris Johnson, who is steeped in the culture of the area, emphasised this to me, 'Being a Catholic

will have marginalised the McMullens, as did being Irish.'

The other marginalising factor was Catherine's illegitimacy, about which, at this point, she herself had no idea. Those who knew she was illegitimate would have had another forceful reason to distance themselves from her. John Atkinson from Brinkburn Street, a mile or so to the east in South Shields, whose sister, Ethel Maud, helped Catherine learn to play the piano in her teens, was in no doubt what people thought about illegitimates: 'Them days people ignored them,' he said. Reny argued that there were 'more illegitimate children than Catherine,' but when I asked her who they were, she could recall only 'Cameron Eckford from the shop… he was illegitimate. He became a sea captain. Belle Eckford was his mother, she married afterwards, a publican.' But Belle had been one of Catherine's few playmates, so her son, Cameron, was not contemporaneous.

In the process of attaining respectability, calling someone a bastard or a drunk was one unanswerable way of showing you were better than them. The precious people of the New Buildings could point to the McMullens with disdain and feel better about themselves.

For his part, John McMullen took every opportunity to puncture what he saw as the bubble of their self-importance, and he had the power to put the fear of God into most people whether he was drunk or sober. Women gossiping at their back doors would disperse when they saw him coming. In an early version of *Our Kate*, Catherine remembered hearing of one angry husband coming to the door and complaining that McMullen had told the his wife to 'get into the family way,' though Catherine doubted that that was the phrase he had used.

Equally, McMullen could hold others in respect, like Arne Fuller, an old friend of his who'd made good. When they bumped into each other one day and Arne invited him for a drink, he bored everyone silly for weeks telling them about it, truly proud that Arne had asked him. He didn't go for the drink, mind.

Once, when the 'house' upstairs came up for rent, a woman arrived with her mother to view it and was instantly recognised by McMullen as a dock prostitute putting on airs and graces. She is supposed to have said that the aspect from the front window was pleasing.

'Arse-pect?' McMullen queried, stoning the plum

in her snooty accent, 'I've got a hen in the backyard with her arse-all-pecked if you want.'

The story brought to Reny's mind another McMullen wickedness: 'We kept some hens and canaries, and one time he stole some corn out of our backyard. He sprinkled it all along the back lane to his yard and our hens followed him. Once he'd got them into his yard, the hens laid their eggs and so the eggs were his. I can't remember it actually happening, but we talked about it.' Such a legend did McMullen become that stories grew up around him that apparently no-one was sure had actually happened.

Rose's first husband, William Fawcett, to whom she was married in the 1870s, had been very different. A quiet, faithful Catholic and stalwart of the Church, he had regular work in the Jarrow shipyard. They had five daughters. When he died of TB, none was yet of working age, and with the workhouse beckoning, Rose took the only job she could find, at the Jarrow Puddling Mills, where pig iron was converted into wrought iron by heating it to very high temperatures. Conditions of work were extremely harsh, wages were very poor, and at one stage they were so hard up they had to beg bread barefoot in Jarrow. The two eldest girls subsequently died at only 13, one before Rose's marriage to their 'saviour', John McMullen, and one about a year afterwards.

Below, Katie's grandfather, William Fawcett. When he died from TB, his five daughters begged barefoot on the streets.

Jack was born soon after Rose married John in 1890, and McMullen found it all he could so to support his new family and stay ahead of the rent man. They moved nine times before Catherine was born in 1906. They had even lived in William Black Street once before. When Rose, John and Jack returned there in 1912 with Katie in tow, Rose was only 54, but she had taken more than she could handle and fell ill that very summer. Five years later, when Katie was 11, she died.

It was a great loss. For the first years, when a child depends on its mother for its physical and emotional needs, Rose had been the one to deliver. Kate hadn't even lived in the same house as her daughter for the first six years of her life, and when she came home on day visits, she was prevented from getting close to the child. One of Katie's earliest memories was being wrested from the arms of her mother by Rose when she came through the front door.

It was agreed, and would prove a terrible mistake, that the McMullen family would live the lie that Kate was not Katie's mother at all, but her sister. That they did this without ever considering that people might question that two sisters should be named Catherine, beggars belief, even in a society where parent and child often took the same first name. 'I was very exercised about this,' said Winnie, 'how two sisters could have the same first name. Given that the McMullens were bringing her up as their own child, it was a very strange thing to do.'

3 UNWANTED SEED

In a story which has so much to do with identity, it is ironic that names are so often confusingly similar. Catherine Cookson (née McMullen) was known as Katie as a child and Kitty as an adult. Her mother, Catherine Fawcett, was known as Kate. I shall refer to them as Catherine and Kate respectively. When, in 1996, I asked Catherine what had led to her leaving the North at the age of 23, she said, 'My answer is there were many reasons, all tangled and representing one word – "rejection"!'

But from Reny I heard that the rejection was not, in the first place, *of* Catherine, but by her: 'She kept herself apart. She rejected everybody.' I put it to Reny that she would only have been aware of Catherine from about 1917/8 (when she was four or five and Catherine was 11 or 12) and that soon after – at 13 – Catherine deliberately cut herself off and took it upon herself to make something of her life, and had she not done so she would never have achieved what she did. But Reny would have none of it: 'It was long before she was 13 that she stopped being a part of things, my dear. As I see it, she was just snobby, you know? And wouldn't bother with anybody. We used to have sing-songs at the top of Simonside Terrace, on the green and my brother used to play the accordion, but she would never join in things like that, never come in

'One time when my father took all the children out in his motorboat, and my brother Bill was learning to steer the boat, Katie jumped up and grabbed his hand. She didn't like him getting the attention, you see. And we bumped one of the big liners we were going to see.'
Reny Harding

Of the few relics of Catherine's childhood, none is so redolent of times past as the great, loose-roped timbers of the dock-side staithes, their design as complex and as geometrically true as the network of threads (thoughts, feelings and emotions) which Catherine pulled from her own early life on Tyneside and out of which were constructed the novels. Before she wrote them, she was an enigma even unto herself.

amongst us. And I remember one time when my father took all the children out in his motorboat, like I told you, and my brother Bill was eleven years older than me, and he was learning to steer the boat one day, Katie jumped up and grabbed his hand. She didn't like him getting the attention, you see. And we bumped one of the big liners we were going to see.

'I'll tell you something else. Katie had gorgeous hair, it was right down her back, beautiful, it had chestnut in, and I was by this time a hairdresser. [Catherine will have been in her mid-twenties.] She came back and she hadn't changed. She came to my shop to have her hair done, not cut or waved because it was wavy. I had to sort of lift her waves up with tongs. She didn't like me having my own shop. You could feel it, you could feel the jealousy! She never came back. She *was* jealous, that was part of her trouble, she was as jealous as sin. I don't know why. My brothers all learned to play the violin, we were a musical family, she tried to learn the violin and she couldn't take it in!'

Talking to Catherine's family I saw that they, too, had found her difficult from an early age. Kate's sister Sarah's children lived in the pit village of Birtley, just south of Gateshead. Aunt Sarah had married a miner, Michael Lavelle, who had been laid off work when he became deaf. 'There were eight of us,' Cousin Sarah told me. 'Mary, Rosie, Bill, Peter (who worked down the pit, and later took Kitty down when she was researching *Maggie Rowan*), twins Michael and Joseph, Kathleen and myself. My father couldn't hear, he had two falls of stone down the pit, but there wasn't any compensation. One child died

[Mary, from TB in her teens], only one and that is to my mother's credit.' Aunt Sarah worked hard, cooking and taking in laundry, and one day the local Roman Catholic priest suggested she might like to take the caretaker's job at the school, 'She said she'd be delighted, so that was income to us.'

Catherine told me that she hadn't enjoyed visiting the Lavelles because, 'Aunt Sarah baked and cooked for selling such as black puddings, and when I was staying there in my young days she sent me to the slaughterhouse for a pint of blood. The very name recalls the picture which makes me feel sick. We never got on. I didn't like her, but I admired her because of the way she worked for that family.'

Now I discovered that she had been 'troublesome' when she went to visit, that Aunt Sarah hadn't warmed to her and that the older Lavelle sisters hadn't liked her either – 'Kitty and my mother never got on,' Cousin Sarah's niece, Rosemary Barker, told me. 'They never liked one another. It was a lot to do with when they were younger. It was from an early age that she was like that, anyway from a teenager.'

I remembered Catherine's own story of how she had been so jealous of Aunt Sarah's Mary, the child who would die from tuberculosis, that when Mary was staying over at William Black Street for the freshness of the air off the river, Catherine actually stole her petticoat. There had been much hunting for the article before Mary's departure, but to no avail. When Kate later found it,

The old pithead at Kibblesworth, high above Birtley, where Catherine's cousins, Aunt Sarah's children, grew up in a far happier environment than she, a family environment of which Catherine became deeply envious, even though she became incapable of accepting love when it was offered to her.

Catherine developed a venomous, deeply destructive streak, which, in the unpublished version of her autobiography, she admits was the reason why she alienated many in the New Buildings: 'I can see myself facing a row of children sitting on a seat that faced the Slacks, a seat that had been placed there for the weary wayfarers travelling between Tyne Dock and Jarrow. I was always the teacher, and I would shout at one, "Spell cat," and if she said, "C.A.T." I would yell, while banging my stick on the ground, "I did not say, 'Spell cat,' I said, 'Spell rat.'" And if she replied, "R.A.T." I would, with more beating, say, "I did not say, 'Spell rat,' I said, 'Spell day.'"

Catherine admitted that she had stolen it out of pure envy and malice: 'I hated the attention she got... I often wished that I could be so bad [ill] that people could make a lot of me.'

Catherine developed a deeply destructive streak and when she visited the Lavelles in Birtley, she would be billeted out with a family nearby. Later she would interpret her exile as self-imposed, to do with 'the black pudding and a little respectful fear of Aunt Sarah,' but just how difficult she became is shown in an early, unpublished version of *Our Kate* (her autobiography), where her malignance is vented on many in the New Buildings: 'I can see myself facing a row of children sitting on a seat that faced the Slacks, a seat that had been placed there for the weary wayfarers travelling between Tyne Dock and Jarrow. I was always the teacher, and I would shout at one, "Spell cat," and if she said, "C.A.T." I would yell, while banging my stick on the ground, "I did not say, 'Spell cat,' I said, 'Spell rat.'" And if she replied, "R.A.T." I would, with more beating, say, "I did not say, 'Spell rat,' I said, 'Spell day.'"

To get to the root of this disruptive, destructive aspect of Catherine's nature, which was what had also nearly caused Billy's early demise beneath the water of the Slake, we must look more closely at the early childhood period, and take into account the period before she was born. For if, as psychologists tell us, our dispositions are shaped by pre-natal events and the birth itself, one shudders to think how John McMullen's terrifying attentions to Kate distorted

Catherine's disposition while yet in her mother's womb. After the birth, there were immediate bonding problems between mother and child. Kate developed mastitis and was unable to breast-feed, and Catherine gives us the disturbing image of McMullen lasciviously sucking Kate's nipples to free the flow of her milk. Then it was decided that the child should be 'left in the care of me granny because Kate had to go out to work again in order to keep me,' and whatever closeness had been achieved between mother and daughter was abruptly curtailed, for Kate slept out in service.

As Catherine's surrogate mother, Rose was, as I have suggested, everything a mother could be, her ample bosom became the child's comforter and the soft, experienced voice of this mature survivor, born before the modern industrial world had got going, was probably Catherine's saving grace. But the salve was only applied after the disruption of Kate's pregnancy and the birth, and the very fact that Catherine's earliest memory was of being wrested from her mother's arms when she came home on a day off suggests an undercurrent of continuing trauma after Kate left.

Catherine was born not in East Jarrow, but at No. 5 Leam Lane, Tyne Dock. The house lay a mile or so to the east, along the Jarrow Road: 'You walked right past the Slake, there was no wall between it and the road,' Reny reminded me, 'and came to the saw mill before you got to the dock itself.' Three hundred yards further, you came to five low, wide, brick arches, over which masses of railway lines ran like spaghetti to the Tyne Dock staithes or

The photograph is dated 1897. It shows the spot where Jarrow Road funnels out into Leam Lane. Catherine was born at No. 5 Leam Lane in June, 1906.

The high retaining wall, close to where the ladies are standing with their parasols, is the start of Tyne Dock, the dock gates being just a short way under the arches in the direction that the ladies are walking.

Looking through the main four arches leading from the Jarrow Road intersection with Leam Lane to the tram terminus and Tyne Dock gates. Catherine would stand beneath one, face the black bricks, close her eyes and let her thoughts roam, sometimes conjuring pictures of a fairytale world which she had no doubt she would one day occupy.

jetties. The first carried waggons to jetties at the north end of the dock, the other four to loading bays at the south end. Just before reaching the first arch, you came to a road leading off to the right, which was Leam Lane and which took you up a hill to the village of Simonside.

On the east side of Leam Lane, as it funnelled out of the Jarrow Road and up towards Simonside, there stood a cluster of buildings – four houses and a pub called The Twenty Seven, the story going that there had once been twenty-six staithes on Tyne Dock and this was the dockers' last port of call. Officially named the Alexander Hotel, and later the Alexandra, the pub occupied the second building on the east side of Leam Lane; the rest being rented houses. The third house along, right next to the pub, was divided into two apartments, numbered 4 and 5. In No. 5, the two-roomed, lower apartment, on June 20, 1906, Katie was born, not as a Fawcett (after her mother), but as a McMullen after her stepgranda.

Being an only child ensured that Catherine was always the object of Rose's attention, and having 'parents' very much older than her gave her an old head on young shoulders – a teacher at school even called her 'Granny'.

Catherine's needs were at the centre of Rose's concerns, and the child developed a cocky, self-orientated personality. Self-protective, but far from self-confident, it described the limits of what Rose had managed to salvage from the dire circumstances of her granddaughter's birth.

The situation did, however, favour the development of the child's natural

intelligence and imagination. Catherine would sit on her grandma's knee and listen to songs and rhymes and stories of old Northumberland lore, which Rose had learned on the knee of her own mother, long before the Tyneside towns of Jarrow and Shields had been fully established.

Winnie remembers, 'Katie was so bright, she was so interested in everything, she was clever... she had these *notions* didn't she?' Other childhood friends were equally impressed by her imagination, one Peggy Chittick remembering a particular occasion when they were playing truant and Catherine spun a tale about the noises a piece of corrugated iron was making on the water, that they encoded dire warnings of what punishments they would receive for staying off school. It had absolutely petrified Peggy.

An essential prerequisite of such an imaginative response to the world is a certain objectivity, a separateness from it, from which state flows an ability to jump one's perceptions out of the mental ruts, formed by experience, into which they normally fall. This feeling of separateness characterised Catherine's childhood and was shared by another writer from the area.

Poet and travel writer James Kirkup was born in South Shields in 1923. He recalls in his autobiography, *A Child of the Tyne*, how in those days it was common to leave a young child out by the front step, crawling around the pavement, 'digging up the thick black dirt between the flagstones. Or I would lie beside the boot-scraper, looking out over the vast, steeply-cambered stretch of cobblestones to the other side of the street…an unknown land where I might

never be allowed to go, where strange children played and people who were not a bit like those on our side of the street went about their business in queer ways.'

Catherine herself described an innate capacity for objective assimilation and associated wonder, and in both cases it was allied to a keen ear for words. James would sometimes bring a word back to his mother: 'Occasionally, I remember, I would go to my mother and whisper in her ear that I had just heard someone say something bad. "What was it?" she would ask, smiling. "I don't like to say it," I would reply. "It was 'bugger'." What a chill of horror used to run through me as I said the awful word!' This is exactly what happened when Catherine first heard the word 'baxtard', which was how she pronounced it when she presented it to her mother later in the day. The tragedy was that it had been used against her by a woman of the New Buildings and meant hurtfully.

The other interesting parallel is that James, like Catherine, was a loner. His one friendship was with a very reserved Japanese girl, who 'did not seem

to belong in our street at all.' He was 'perfectly happy in my own company,' and when he did venture beyond the family circle he became impatient with the inadequacy of the other children. He found them 'alarming, noisy and dull, and I used to wave to them, in what I think was a perfectly friendly manner. I certainly had no desire to join them, or imitate their childish ways.'

Is this what the New Buildings children disliked about Catherine, and a part of the reason why they thought her snobby? Did some of them perhaps feel threatened by it? For Reny and her sister were wholly *of* the New Buildings community, inseparable from it, and Catherine, from the start, was a person apart. This feeling of apartness she once described to me as one of 'aloneness, in opposition to loneliness – there is a great difference between the two.' Part of it is a sense of imaginative autonomy, which in Catherine's case came to bind together so many loose threads of her psyche.

Unfortunately, being 'a thing apart' will not make the writer popular in a playground culture on an estate like the New Buildings, especially if the child is unpractised in the give-and-take of sibling rivalry, as Catherine was when she arrived. Leam Lane End was a cut-through community, quite unlike the self-contained, island community of the New Buildings. Street play was a novelty to her, aged 6, and it would have been unwise to celebrate her coming

Said Reny, 'Skippy ropes and ball are the games we used to play,' Skipping rope on long summer evenings to a ritualistic chanting of rhymes was particularly popular among the bigger girls. James Kirkup recalls feeling 'a little uneasy' about the first time he witnessed 'a crowd of girls dancing in a ring round the lamp-post near our door, singing the rhyme at the tops of their voices… – something rather wild about the words and the abandon of the dancing faintly shocked my infant primness; and on the final word, the girls all lifted up their frocks at the back and shoved their bottoms out in a way which I found very distressing.'

by taking a leading role, which is, I suspect, what this less than confident, but sparky little girl did.

There is, of course, a big difference between the sense of distance and 'aloneness' that Kirkup and Catherine describe and the malignant jealousy and snobbiness of which she stands accused by Reny and, indeed, by her family, but perhaps one is a kind of damaged version of the other.

Unlike Catherine, James Kirkup was part of a happy, loving family: 'My father and mother had a hard life in harsh surroundings, but from early childhood I can remember much laughter and true happiness,' he wrote. 'They must have taken great pains to conceal from me the financial difficulties they suffered.' So, James was secure in his relationship with his parents and could release any tensions caused by his standoffishness by flinging himself into his mother's arms, crying and laughing and offering no explanation for doing so, because none was ever required of him.

For Catherine that simply wasn't possible because just after the move to East Jarrow, Rose fell ill, Kate was brought home to take up the reins of the household, and the dissemblance over who her parents really were was exposed, causing the child to 'freeze up' psychologically. This was the crucial determiner. Suddenly, the veil of security that had been drawn over the sub-

Kate, Catherine's mother, aged about forty and already bloated with drink. Ten years earlier, when Rose fell ill, she came home to her daughter and Catherine found it impossible suddenly to accept her. In earlier times, when Kate arrived on rare days off, if she attempted to cuddle Catherine, Rose would grab the child from her and dust down her clothes, as if Kate might contaminate her. Kate's sister, Sarah, said that she drank to drown her sorrows, the principal one being a daughter who hated her.

conscious fears that had shaped Catherine's disposition since before she was born, was lifted, and all the things that 'people were thinking underneath the niceness', as Catherine put it, were shown to be real. For the little girl, whose cockiness betrayed a deep-down unsureness, it was a shattering experience.

After school, the streets of this tiny, island community came alive, for people made their own amusements then. John Atkinson remembers: 'We used to play at the backlane – football, cricket. We were good lads. Go to bed about 11 o'clock. We'd play out in the dark under the gas lights. Parents would have their neighbours in, all sorts. Our house was the main place in the street for entertainment like, on account of the piano, which my sister played.'

Said Reny, 'Skippy ropes and ball are the games we used to play,' and Winnie remembers a brick recess for a fireplace and chimney on the outside wall of her house as one focal point for games: 'The outside chimney – we used to like to hide in there.'

On this particular evening in 1913, the girls were playing a game of shops in this outside-wall, chimney recess. Whether Winnie was there isn't clear, probably not, she was only 3. Reny was not yet born. Almost certainly Florrie, her sister, will have been in attendance.

All of a sudden, someone snitched Catherine's 'boody', a piece of glass used as money in the game of shops. She challenged the culprit, threatening to tell her da. The girl retaliated with the news that Catherine 'ain't go no da,' that John McMullen wasn't her da, that Rose wasn't her ma, and that her real ma was her 'sister', Kate.

How completely this news devastated Catherine has been told countless times, and Catherine herself described the incident and one that followed two years later – her exclusion from a birthday party in Philipson Street – as the springboard for all her problems, often giving the impression that the shame of illegitimacy was to blame.

She *will* have felt ashamed, because illegitimacy was a big black mark in the respectability game culture, as John Atkinson said. But what really shook the little girl was the information that Rose and John were not her parents. The web of security that Rose had spun was shown to be a web of lies. Catherine had lost her real mother at birth, and she would not be restored to her until the last few years of Kate's life, but now it had been shown that Rose was not her mother either. Love had disposed of her. This was her real trauma.

After hours of picking at the flaking whitewash on the inside wall of the backyard lavatory of No. 10, Catherine's whole world seemed to have disintegrated into a scattering of lies at her feet.

Even her feeling of being 'a thing apart', her imaginative autonomy, was corrupted by fear. For the first time she attached fear to being alone, 'and this was *deep* inside me and I shall always be lonely. I can be jolly. I can be the life and soul of the party, but I can understand these men who are always very jolly and go and commit suicide.'

Thus she set the episode in the chimney piece on the outside wall of the Richardsons' house as an early, significant event in a train which, thirty years later, would bring her to the gates of a Herefordshire mental asylum and indeed subsequently to attempted suicide.

The episode froze her in her tracks. Normally, a child is eased gently out of its shell of dependency on its mother. Child development is a gradual process away from the self-centred, narcissistic state of dependence on a mother figure, to independence, integrity and freedom. For Catherine, this process was in an instant curtailed, the emotional 'umbilical cord', connecting her to a mother's love, was not so much severed as shown not to exist, and she responded by refusing the love of this woman, Kate, whom she could not accept as a mother, and who had earlier rejected her.

'Kate was never a mother to me,' Catherine snarled into my tape recorder only seven years ago. 'She didn't know how to be a mother. Kate was never made to be a mother, and the fact is nor did I *want* her to be my mother.'

Catherine never loved her mother and from this moment on, she found difficulty in forming affective attachments to anyone. Her relationships became bound up with an obsessive preoccupation with her own needs, in particular a deeply felt, existential need to prove her own worth. In this she was swimming in the shallows of a stream called 'autism', where the strongest mid-stream currents have its victims struggling against any demand for human, social contact, unless manipulation can take place.

In the first, unpublished draft of *Our Kate*, Catherine states that it was after the chimney-piece episode, that 'the fight started within me'.

Cut off from feeling she set out like a wounded animal aggressively to meet her needs on her own, but the aggression was not just about self-preservation, it had this malignant aspect – there were strong feelings of bitterness and hate involved, which readers know only too well from the tone and many incidents in the novels.

When I spoke to Catherine about the cruelty, bitterness and hate in books such as *A Dinner of Herbs* or *The Whip*, where torture is gratuitously involved, or *Feathers in the Fire*, where it is present with a sadistic connotation, she acknowledged straight away that it was part of her own character, but traced it back only to 1945, to her breakdown: 'When you have a nervous breakdown,' she said, 'you come out with a different attitude. You never get rid of a breakdown. The sediment of it lies in your subconscious. An incident, a word, or even a place can stir that sediment again and there you are back. In my case it is aggression, deep aggression against my early suffering, against my mother... I learned how to hate, to hate with such intensity that I knew if I let it have the upper hand I knew that my future life would be ruined. The feelings have stayed with me. It's the *feelings* that come out in different stories...'

Those feelings started in embryo here, in the New Buildings.

In *Our Kate* she tells how aggressive she became with the other children, bossing, bullying and slapping, needing to 'play lead' in any game she undertook, insisting on being in charge, enacting the 'Eeny, meeny, miny

Croft Terrace, where Kate took in laundry and one day Catherine returned it, regaling her mother's employers with stories of how she punched and slapped the other children down. On the way home that day she hung on the back of a coal cart while the man wasn't looking and saved the penny she would have spent on the tram. Arriving back much later than expected, she had her ears boxed by Kate.

mo' selection in a game of 'deady-one' in the chimney piece of Winnie's house by stabbing her finger viciously into the chest of each unfortunate player as the rhyme did its rounds.

Suddenly, she was 'bent on showing them; showing the lot of them.' It was during this period that she nearly drowned Billy in the Slake, that she hit a girl in the street and and stole her skipping rope, that she regularly berated her class of children about how to spell 'cat'. This is the period in which she embarked upon a strategy so destructive that parents turned up in umbrage at the front door of No. 10 with alarming regularity.

The change of tack clearly came as something of a shock to some, including the children of a large Scottish family called Ween or Weir (the name differs as to which manuscript you read), who lived above Catherine's great-aunt Maggie, Rose's sister, at No. 26 William Black Street. Normally it was the Weir boys who did the chasing, now they turned tail whenever they saw Catherine coming.

The delinquency came out of the hurt, and Kate got it all terribly wrong, boxing her ears or spanking her, which just made matters worse. In her novel, *The Maltese Angel*, when Fanny asks her daughter, Jessie, how she expects people to love her when she is so naughty, little Jessie replies that she is naughty *because* nobody loves her and never has. This is so very important in attempting to understand Catherine's personality. Love had deserted and disposed of her at a very early age, and virtually everything follows from that.

Party girl with no party to go to. The absence of an invitation was hardly surprising, but a devastating blow.

In an early draft, Catherine tells how Kate took in laundry from a woman in Croft Terrace, Jarrow. She'd get Catherine to carry a basket of washing from Dee Street (where the tram from the New Buildings dropped her) to the woman's address in Croft Terrace. It was 'a large washing basket, over which I could just stretch my arms. To carry it from Dee Street right up to Croft Terrace was a test almost beyond my strength. Yet on one of these excursions I remember the owner of the washing walking with me towards Dee Street. She had a friend with her and she was going to some meeting, and I regaled them with stories of my achievements in the fighting line. I told them I could beat anybody in the New Buildings, and I gave them a demonstration of how I punched and slapped. They shook their heads and laughed. I was a queer little thing, no doubt they thought.'

They laughed, but Catherine was embarked on a truly destructive strategy and inevitably, just two years after the chimney-breast revelation, it led to another

episode of total misery. 'I wasn't a great pal of Cecilia Walker but I was about the same age [later she inserted the phrase, "and I played with her"], and I knew she was going to have a birthday party and the last time I remembered a party was when I lived at Leam Lane…'

Parties were far from common, and to Catherine they seemed like magical events. 'Once you were invited to a party, *everything* changed. Life was wonderful, a fairyland forever and ever more… And now Cecilia Walker was to have a party. As we played in the Back Lane we talked about it; this one's going, that one's going. Florrie Harding, Joan Woodcock, Lottie Christopher, Olive Swinburn, names come rolling back to me, they were all going to the party, and I was going to the party, of course I was.'

But no invitation arrived.

Kate tried to put her off going, but Catherine stood at the back door and went anyway. 'I found myself knocking on the bottom of the staircase door. There is a blessed veil drawn over my encounter with whoever came down to answer the door, for the next thing I remembered I was walking straight across from the Walkers to our back door. I can see myself going up the yard and into the kitchen, and as I stood near the table with my fingers in my mouth gnawing at my nails, I remember Kate saying, "You're the wrong colour, hinny." Colour in this case referred to religion, not nationality, and then she added, "Don't worry, your day will come, as will mine." How true, how true.'

What is so interesting is that in this first version of the story, written in the mid-1950s, the person whom she meets on the stairs is not designated as a child and does not give the reason for her exclusion as, 'You ain't go not da,' which is the legend Catherine later perpetuated. There is no mention of her illegitimacy at all. Instead, religion is the discriminator, as it is in her novel, *Colour Blind*.

The point is that Catherine was an outsider, she had been alienated by her own society. She could only face this if she could show prejudice on the part of others in the business. It is not unlike John McMullen's response to his detractors. But her omission from the party list had nothing to do with prejudice, either against Catholics or against illegitimates, it had to do with her incapacity to make friends.

In the 1970s, when Catherine returned to the site of William Black Street, which had just been demolished, she posed at the back door of the house on Philipson Street where the party had taken place, still unable fully to comprehend what had happened. It was years before she could accept why her people had rejected her.

About this time, Kate co-opted Catherine on two regular chores, fetching beer from the off licence or pub and, on a Monday morning instead of going to school, taking a parcel to Bob Gompertz, the pawnbroker on Bede Street, Tyne Dock. The beer was fetched in a stone jar called the Grey Hen, made for holding vinegar, but ideal for carrying pulled pints. Catherine tells us how she took it 'even as far as Brinkburn Street in Stanhope Road' [maybe two miles] to have it filled. John Atkinson tells me that the 'outdoor beer shop in Brinkburn Street was called Pratts, on the corner, right to the bottom on the other side from where I lived. He used to serve bottles of beer and anything like that. You could get a pint pulled, loose beer. I used to go for it when I was younger. You'd pull it into a can.'

In later life Catherine cited these chores as reason for resentment. On the face of it, she had a point. Kate made her stay off school to go to the pawn often enough to court legal action, and what is really unforgivable is that it was a wilful denial of so much promise. As Winnie noted, 'Katie was so bright, she was so interested in everything, she was clever...' All that was being wasted by her mother. Again, Catherine tells of the shame she felt carrying her bundle to the pawn, walking past the dockers lining up at the shipping offices at Tyne Dock. Margaret Hargreaves remembered the sad huddle outside Gompertz's on a Monday morning – 'a small group of women waiting at Bob's pawn shop with their bundles, they used to say their bundles were their men folk's suits, which had been taken out of pawn on Saturday and were taken back to pawn on the Monday.' Catherine would have been among them.

She wasn't the only one going for beer, and Reny Harding remembers her sister Florrie escorting Catherine to the Alkali pub on the Jarrow Road, but it was clearly not something to be proud of. Florrie was under express instruction never actually to go in. Nevertheless, typically, Catherine soon turned these chores to advantage.

Kate must have had her reasons for sending Catherine to different beer shops and pubs, some of them miles away, and it may well have been that she was running up a tab at a number of them at the same time. What it certainly meant was that she felt bound to give Catherine a halfpenny for the tram ride back if she was sending her all the way into Tyne Dock, for a grey hen, full to capacity, was heavy – it took about two shillings to fill, which represented quite a few pints. Those halfpennies became Catherine's profit margin. She would opt to struggle back with the heavy jug, balanced on her

The Alkali pub (above), where Catherine was sent to fetch Kate's beer, is still serving today.

As the picture opposite shows, Catherine was not the only child to be sent on such an errand.

hip, save the tram fare and store the coins in various hidey holes, the favourite one of which was her 'bank' in the rafters of the backyard lavatory.

In time, Kate rumbled what was going on and, when she was short, would ask in a pathetic voice if Catherine had a few coppers to spare, which cannot have gained her much respect in her daughter's eyes.

So business-like did Catherine become in this that she began to arrange things so that Kate would send her to a particular beer shop in Lord Nelson Street, off Hudson Street, not far from the dock. There were three outdoor beer shops there, so she could appear to be ringing the changes while always visiting a favourite one that was run by an elderly woman, 'the reason being that at least once a week she gave me the wrong change and always to my advantage.'

Another bonus of these trips was that they took her deep into dockland, beneath the arches opposite Leam Lane End and past the actual dock gates. Everyone who lived in the vicinity before the mid-1970s, when they

were destroyed, remembers these arches. 'We used to think they were wonderful,' said Reny, 'They carried the railway lines on top, but the drips, the greasy drips… well, my clothes were a mess from them.'

To Catherine, these 'five slime-dripping arches' were subterranean caves, full of mystery. Entering them was like entering the Underworld, and her fancy took flight. She would stand still, face the black bricks, close her eyes and let her thoughts roam, sometimes conjuring pictures of a fairytale world which she had no doubt she would one day occupy.

Beyond the arches she would follow the high dock wall to the actual dock gates and the tram terminus. The tram actually stopped here for the first time only a few days after Catherine was born, although the place had long been a point of entry, for it was the site of the original Toll Gate.

Now, in Catherine's day, about twenty feet from the police box that guarded the dock gates, 'a man would take a pole and turn the long overhead leads round to

To Catherine, these five slime-dripping arches were subterranean caves, full of mystery. Entering them was like entering the Underworld, and her fancy took flight.

what had been the back of the car and link it to the wires above. Passengers for their return journey would be standing against the iron railings that bordered the dock shipping offices.' As Catherine said to me, 'The tram terminus seemed to be a full stop between East Jarrow and Tyne Dock. From this point Shields seemed to begin.'

Terminus was the Roman god of boundaries, and here the wider world began, and the industry that served it was undertaken. Here, too, she soaked in so much of the spirit of these times that found their way into the early novels. The site of the dock gate terminus regularly appears some forty-five pages in as the background to some crucial scene.

When her granda was on a double shift she used to meet him with his lunch at the dock gates, usually carrying a traditional pot pie, tied up in a red bait handkerchief. He'd come out to collect it, his moleskin trousers red to above the knees from the iron ore that he had been separating from clay and shovelling out of the hold of some ship from Bilbao.

It was never 'Bilbao' that the men said, but 'Bilbo', and they would talk iron ore and pit props, and call this double shift 'turning the boat round'. While she waited for her granda to duck out for his bait, Catherine stood by the police box that guarded the big dock gates and watched the waggons coming off the

Tyne Dock staithes, loaded with ore.

The terminus of the Jarrow car was but twenty feet from this police box. Opposite, Hudson Street led up a steep bank bordered on one side by public houses leading up from Slake Terrace and on the other by the shipping offices and railings, against which, besides the tram passengers for the return journey into Jarrow, men would line up to be picked for jobs on the boats. When Catherine was young these railings were black with men waiting to be set on, all kinds of men, top men, trimmers, crane men, the lot. John McMullen took his place among them. Although he drank, he was a good worker and was nearly always picked for a boat if one was in. Up the steep bank past the bars and shipping offices you came to the Crown Cinema, where occasionally Catherine would attend a Saturday matinée, St Peter & Paul's church and school, and on to the railway station.

John Atkinson, born in nearby Brinkburn Street in 1917, remembers, 'It was very busy then, full of ships, it attracted people from all over the place. There was all sorts, Philippinos, these six, seven footers, Ceylonese, they were seamen, wore big brimmed hats…

'When you came to the gates, you turned round and right in front of you were the beer bars on Slake Terrace, the Empress, the Neptune and the Grapes and all 'em were there. There was a café, Kennedy's, and Café Norj. Where the café was, there was a big flight of stairs up into Dock Street. And the pawn shop was up there [Bede Street], up these stairs. There were clubs up Hudson Street, too, and when the men poured out through the dock gates, the pints were all ready on the counters for them. There'd be trouble up there many a time.'

The 'modern' traffic of the 1960s invades the famous Tyne Dock arches, a place of mystery and imagination for Catherine as a child.

Looking from the dock gates (bottom right) through the first of the Tyne Dock arches towards East Jarrow. Hudson Street leads off to the left and the dock bank with the line of pubs is behind camera.

The first three novels to be written – *Kate Hannigan, Kate Hannigan's Girl* (withdrawn by Catherine after an inexplicably lukewarm reception by the publishers and only recently published) and *The Fifteen Streets*, all treat this terminus point, the heart of docklands, this full stop between Shields and East Jarrow, as a significant *locus*.

In the first two, around page 40, depending on the edition you are using, it is given virtually the same treatment. Catherine is mapping the area for the reader from this point. Kate Hannigan passes through the dock arches and stands waiting for a tram beyond the dock gates, opposite the dock offices and line of pubs. She describes the groups of dockers hoping to be taken on, and notes their hierarchy. She points out short-trousered coolies with bass bags

The Jarrow tram coming to a halt at the dock gates.

stuffed with fish knocking against their thin legs, and large bodied sea captains and sailors from all parts of the world. The scene is wholly alive with vivid impressions from the author's youth, as heads are turned towards her and remarks passed. Fifty or more pages further on, we are back in the same spot with Annie Hannigan, Kate's daughter who is interchangeable with Catherine as a child, but now we are entering from a different direction.

Annie approaches the dock gates on a tram from smart Westoe Village to the east, entering Tyne Dock via Bolden Lane and Hudson Street (still there today). The tram rolls past Stanhope Road, St Peter & Paul's church and school, on past the station and the roads running off Hudson Street to the right: Lord Nelson Street, Bede Street (where the pawn shop was) and Dock Street (only Lord Nelson Street leads off it today) and on, down the dock bank, past the line of pubs, before stopping opposite the wall behind which the dock horses were stabled. Annie alights from the tram and waits at the terminus for her ma.

It is indeed a significant place and a significant moment, for Annie has just learned that Kate, whom she

had always thought of as her sister, is in fact her ma.

This time the scene is perfected with an eye not just for descriptive detail, but for environment as plot. Annie stands watching the assortment of nationalities, but then picks out a boy pressed with his back against the railings of the dock offices apparently waiting for a tram. She discovers that in fact he is also waiting for his ma, who is drinking in one of the pubs opposite. He tells her proudly that he has got a penny and shows it to her, pressed deep into the flesh of his hand on account of his grasping the iron railings behind him. Annie laughs and gives him another, asking him what he will buy with his wealth. He tells her that he'll get himself a pork dip or a pie and peas.

At that point, two other characters come into the picture, a whippet called Earl and a man, who has overheard the boy and tells us the dog likes his food also, going to prove his point by pouring a bottle of spirits down the skinny, shivering creature's throat. It makes the boy laugh, but Annie withdraws, repelled, as she remembers others of the dog's breed tearing rabbits apart, coursing on open ground at East Jarrow.

Suddenly the boy looks up and sees his mother, lurching, reeling drunk out of the pub with a man, whose hands are all over her breasts. As Annie watches, she realises with horror and shame that the woman is Kate's cousin Connie, who proceeds to foul mouth the boy and demand to know who gave him a penny. When he tells her, Connie turns on Annie with her bloodshot eyes and she is filled with a nameless terror.

In the third novel, *The Fifteen Streets*, Catherine leads us through the area once more, this time in the company of Katie O'Brien, who is participating in another of Catherine's 'shames' as a child, she is carrying a parcel of clothes from East Jarrow to the pawn shop in Bede Street. We accompany her through the dock arches and past the dock gates, where she meets moth-eaten old Mrs Flaherty, who always saw little Katie's potential and is astounded that she has been kept off school yet again.

Thus does Catherine pack into three passages so many of her own feelings and emotions – about her own mother, about the tasks she sets that shame her, about the hopelessness of her own situation. Thus, too, does she demonstrate how those feelings became a part of her

To go to the pawnshop with any parcel filled Katie O'Brien with shame in The Fifteen Streets, just as it did Catherine in real life. She knew that the men idling against the railings of the dock offices were watching her as she turned off into Bede Street, where the pawn shop was, and if she met any of her school mates she would almost die with shame.

early environment, and gave her stories their light and shade.

There is a Dickensian feel about this period of Catherine's life. For Charles Dickens wandered the streets of London from 8 or 9, also alone, because his parents were in the Marshalsea prison. He, too, suffered 'unreasoning terrors', and with 'a feeling of dismal dignity' upon him would sit down 'on a step to consider how to get through life.' As Catherine, he would stand and stare at busy intersections – the dock gates for Catherine were Seven Dials, Covent Garden, for the young Dickens – 'What wild visions of prodigies of wickedness, want, and beggary, arose in my mind out of that place!' he wrote. He also described himself as 'a queer little thing' and, like Catherine, claimed to have suffered and 'suffered exquisitely'.

Dickens' fears and terrors shaped the environments of his youth, just as Catherine's fears shaped hers, his young life being lived on such a diet of imaginative fare that not only did these 'living environments' become significant *loci* in the novels, but actual events that contained his feelings also flooded them, as here in *David Copperfield*. It could be Catherine fetching Kate's beer:

I was such a child, and so little, that frequently when I went into the bar of a strange public house, they were afraid to give it me. I remember one hot evening... The landlord looked at me over the bar, from head to foot, with a strange smile on his face; and instead of drawing the beer, looked round the screen and said something to his wife. She came out from behind it, with her work in her hand, and joined him in surveying me... They asked me a good many questions; as, what my name was, how old I was, where I lived, how I was employed, and how I came there. To all of which... I invented, I am afraid, appropriate answers. They served me with the ale, though I suspect it was not the Genuine Stunning; and the landlord's wife, opening the little half door of the bar, and bending down, gave me my money back, and gave me a kiss that was half admiring and half compassionate, but all womanly and good, I am sure.

The imaginative stimulus Catherine drew indirectly from her wanderings did nothing to ameliorate her utterly negative feelings about being Kate's daughter. It was as if she needed to pit herself against Kate in retaliation for the hurt that had been dealt her, as if she held Kate responsible for the mess of her birth and the absence of love in her life. For the fact was that Catherine could not love her mother, she felt only antagonism and hate, which she now brought to ground in Kate's dependence on alcohol, a dependence which may well have been precipitated by her daughter's antagonism.

Drunkenness was an endemic problem of the region. In a survey of the whole country, Lancashire and the North East were far and away the worst offenders. These were the areas of worker concentration. In Lancashire, the cotton industry was paramount, in the North East it was coal, iron, steel, ship building, as well as other industries, such as chemicals, glass, pottery, and paper. In both areas, alcohol reduced a large portion of the work force to slavery. Employers owned the pubs and many of the houses in which their workers lived. In some cases they got the wages back even before the rent could be paid.

Just how much a problem drunkenness was locally is demonstrated by the Court reports in the *Shields*

Gazette on June 20, 1906, the day Catherine was born. A fisherman called Kain, who lived with his wife and children in Hudson Street was charged for wilfully assaulting his child by scalding him. The man was drunk and upset the kettle on his wife and baby. When the Chief Constable went to the house, he found the mother drunk in bed with the badly scalded child. The father was also drunk, sitting in the kitchen by the fire, and 'appeared to be indifferent' when asked if he didn't think the child should be taken to hospital. Later, in court, their 17-year-old daughter, Sarah Kain, testified that neither her father nor her mother were drunk on the night in question. Mr Kain was given a four month sentence. The child died.

The hard drinking docker culture was to blame for untold misery.

Before the Bench on this same day, were a drunk charged with throwing an orange from the gallery of the Empire Theatre at a music hall artiste, a smuggler from North Shields, a pork butcher called Jos Reidl, who, whenever he was in drink, struck his wife many times and chased her out of the house, a miner called Miles Lewins, who was fined five shillings for being drunk in charge of a horse and flat (cart) in Coronation street, fourteen youths accused of wilful damage, a woman called Jane Revell, who was given six months for neglecting her six children in what is described as 'a most filthy house'. Her husband 'had been obliged to leave the woman through her bad habits… Since he had left her he had allowed her £1 a week, and that money had been spent on drink.' Finally, thirty-five-year-old Sarah Jane Smart was summoned for neglecting her two children. Her husband gave her between 32 and 36 shillings a week and described her as 'not a sober woman', she pawned her family's clothes and 'frequently kept the boy away from school to look for cinders.'

Kate never sent Catherine to look for cinders on the slag heaps, though she often went on her own accord. But many other aspects strike a chord – the pawned clothes, the drinking and keeping off school. Neither Reny's mother nor Winnie's went this way, so no wonder that Catherine felt ashamed of hers.

In *Our Kate*, she describes how one day she came out of the Crown Cinema in Hudson Street, walking happily down the dock bank towards the arches, when she saw Kate coming from the direction of Bede Street. This must be the inspiration for the scene described above in *Kate Hannigan*, where Annie is faced with the disturbing vision of the drunken Connie, her mother's cousin. This time it is Catherine's own mother, for real, who weaves her way across the road, dragging her left foot behind her and talking in a befuddled fashion.

It is the first time that Catherine saw her mother drunk and the first of many times she felt sick to her chest when she was so.

Catherine came to dread there being money to spare in the house because then Kate would take herself off to the pub and drink not beer but whisky. Her excursions were mostly given to Friday and Saturday, and Catherine came to dread Fridays so much that she approached the house with her hands together in prayer.

Kate at this time, top row, right.

People would stop her in the street and say, 'What's the matter, Katie, are you cold?'

The repulsion she felt at the smell of whisky on Kate's breath when she came to kiss her was enough to turn her stomach over, and she remembered one terrible occasion in particular when she pushed Kate away with the flat of her hand and told her repeatedly through clenched teeth that she hated her. Kate staggered back, clearly deeply hurt.

What compounded Catherine's distress further was that almost everyone else seemed to love Kate. She once admitted that no-one hated Kate except her and Aunt Mary. (Mary is supposed to have been jealous of Kate's popularity, particularly with Alec, her husband, and did everything to overreach her.)

Winnie gave me a wholly credible description of how the other kids saw Kate: 'The mother, Kate, was a very nice person. Maybe she was always drunk, I don't know. Perhaps she was in disgrace. We didn't know about that, only that we could take tatey peelings to the door to feed her hens and she would give us a sweet, you know? She was mad, she was always cracking jokes, she made a great fuss of children. She was a nice person.'

Catherine's family was horrified when they read,

in 1969, what she had written about her mother in *Our Kate*. With telling understatement, Teri, Aunt Mary's daughter, said, 'The reaction was a little bit of shock in certain places that she could talk about Kate in this way.'

If they had read the unpublished version of Catherine's autobiography, written eleven years earlier and more pointedly entitled *From The Seed All Sorrow*, they would have got the full taste of her bile.

Earlier, on a trip north from Hastings, which by this time she had made her home, Catherine was left in no doubt as to whose side the family was on.

'Sarah, I know, was so proud to have a famous cousin and she did me well with a beautiful tea,' Catherine told me. 'Then they were all in her sitting room talking about the family and all saying how they had liked Aunt Kate. "Oh wasn't Aunt Kate a joker. She was the best practical joker that ever lived." And if I hated Kate for nothing else I hated her for her awful practical jokes. "How merry she was. How kind she was. Always had a welcome when you went to see her. And the life and soul of any party." On and on it went and then quite quietly I said, "Yes, Kate was all that, I know. But then you hadn't to live with her. You didn't know the other side." Like a shot of a gun one of the sons [Michael, one of Sarah's twin brothers] sprang up and said, "Don't you dare say a word about my Aunt Kate. You're not fit to wipe her shoes." Imagine the silence that followed. My poor cousin Sarah didn't know where to put herself… And since then I've hated that fellow. Not only was he the first person who had ever insulted me in public and belonging to the family. From that day I disowned [him] in my mind, although as my fortunes progressed I helped them wherever most needed. And even *he* had the nerve to write and ask me for money! I have never felt spiteful against anyone in my life, but I felt it against that man and still do.'

Of course, there are people who drink and pull down those around them while seeming to others, who perhaps see them only occasionally, to be the life and soul of the party, and it may be that Kate was one thing to Catherine, who was with her in a very confined space every day, and another to those who turned up for parties and drunken sing-songs, of which there were many when Kate took lodgers in.

These lodgers, who might come six at a time –

In the 3-roomed house on William Black Street there was no escape for Catherine when lodgers descended, and it's not difficult to imagine how overpowering this sudden influx of rowdy, steamy masculinity was to a young, impressionable girl.

they'd pile in with Jack in the bedroom, Kate and Catherine would sleep in the kitchen – were often men who'd been at sea for a few months, sometimes for as long as two years. With money no object and reverie felt to be deserved, there'd be drinking and raucous sing-songs, and Kate came into her own at the centre of it all.

Catherine cringed at the transformation of her mother into the slack-jawed saloon girl when she was high. Worse still, many of the men fancied their chances with her.

'Kate would flirt,' I was told. 'She was flirtatious, she would flirt with anything that walked in in trousers quite honestly.' On one occasion in Birtley, when a local headmaster was there, 'Kate was flirting away with him and they literally had to take her off to bed – you know, get her away or there's going to be trouble.'

Years earlier, when Catherine was a child, there were no headmasters to be seen at No 10. Most of Kate's lodgers were rough, coarse, simple men, albeit often kind underneath. Competing for Kate's favours were regulars like docker Billy Potts, who'd smuggle out grain for her in his trousers, tied below the knees, the young, more romantic figure of Dick Cartner, an agitator who sounded the sonorous chimes of political unrest that would lead to the General Strike of 1926, and a huge sea captain, who smelt of mothballs and brine. Another regular was a stoker called David McDermott, who first arrived in a long-haul gang, brought up from the docks by Uncle Jack.

There is no doubt that Kate did develop a serious drink problem. Aunt Sarah used to say that she drank methylated spirits as well, and when she arrived at the Lavelle family home in Birtley, they used to have to hide the drink away. Indeed, there was a serious falling out after Kate turned up drunk to the funeral of the teenage TB victim, Mary Lavelle. The rift lasted years before the two sisters buried the hatchet – 'Kate came round the path one day,' remembers Cousin Sarah, 'she came to see my mum, to put things right. Kate was very kind, very good-hearted, but my mother always said she drank to drown her sorrows.'

But it is likely, too, that Kate's biggest sorrow was the fact that she knew what her daughter felt about her. Even Catherine had been disturbed by Kate's look of utter disconsolation when she told Kate she hated her, and years later she acknowledged that she may have been too harsh. All her life she fancied she could rumble Kate when she was lying to her about whether she'd been drinking. She'd give a little laugh, a dry cough, to cover the lie up. Years later, when she was lying ill and hadn't touched a drop for months, Catherine heard that

Catherine, aged 12, second from right, middle row, the photo taken near William Black Street in 1918.

same little cough again, and felt 'a tinge of remorse'.

Perhaps repulsion at Kate's drinking was one way Catherine could justify her inability to love her mother. And it was an absolute inability – 'It broke Katie's heart,' said Winnie with poignant insight, 'because, you know, she *wanted* to love her mother. And when she was at home and she was going out to work, she'd be walking along the road towards Tyne Dock and her mother would bring out a little stool and put it in the porch. She stood on the stool to give her more height – and they'd be waving to each other all the way along. Katie would stop and wave to her mother, she was smiling all the time. All the time she was waving at her mother she'd be laughing at her as well. This didn't happen when she was going on holiday, this happened when she was going out to work! Katie was very fond of her mother. It was a great pity and a great heartbreak for her not to be able to love her.'

Nobody, other than Winnie, saw that.

As Catherine herself said to me, 'I was to learn that hate and bitterness were two emotions that can wipe out love,' and by the time she reached her thirties, she was incapable of it: 'Part of me was as cold as marble.'

4 WHITE LIGHT

A short walk to the north-west of the New Buildings, close to the site of a Roman fort, lies another significant *locus* – St Paul's Monastery, Jarrow, which sits at the opposite pole to the destructive power of the Slake in Catherine's early life.

Here, in this remote corner of the North East of England, the Venerable Bede (673-735 AD) inspired the spread of Christianity throughout Western Europe, and some time later Catherine made her first Confession and received Communion.

Religion has long offered man relief from the burden of 'becoming man', and it served Catherine with a much-needed sense of unity within. It also gave her a new family, for always she prayed to the Holy Family, never directly to God.

As a teenager, she went to Church twice on Sunday, said her prayers each day, went to Confession as often as once a week and erected an altar in her bedroom. Always since she was a child she had had an altar in the room where she slept. It consisted of a black crucifix on an iron stand, a statue of Our Lady with the Infant Child in her arms, another of St Joseph, and a glass Holy Water bottle. At home she set it up on the little iron mantelpiece in the corner of the room she shared with Kate. Only the presence of lodgers (in which case she and Kate had to share a temporary bed in the kitchen) would prevent her saying her prayers night and day beside it. Even at 18, when she went to live and work at Harton Workhouse, she set up her altar.

What she sensed in religion was the power to unify her fractured psyche, and, in a vision, she would receive her first real feeling of pure, selfless love, for which she so yearned, but could neither give nor find. How characteristic of the drama of her life that this should be sourced in so deep a spiritual well as St Paul's Monastery, Jarrow. In *The Blind Miller*, she gives its founder the ultimate accolade, cutting out St Bede as the original Tynesider, someone who had pushed himself up by his own efforts, although in fact Bede had been attached to a monastery as a young boy.

In her childhood, his monastery was the focus of a small mining community. It

St Paul's Monastery, Jarrow, from which the Venerable Bede inspired the spread of Christianity throughout Western Europe.

Here, too, Catherine made her first Confession and received her first Communion.

was also associated with St Bede's School, Jarrow, which Catherine attended for three years from 1913, before she moved to the Catholic school of St Peter & Paul, Tyne Dock. Once ensconced at St Bede's, her indoctrination in the tenets of Roman Catholicism proceeded apace. In this the Church succeeded because it found her where no-one else did: in her imagination. 'The missionaries used to visit the churches in the North periodically to stimulate the faithful, revive the flagging and put the fear of God in the devotees.' She said that she never found God: 'I was borne to Him on the burning shovel of a zealous missionary.

'I was brought up to believe that Sunday was God's day. He had that for himself. And on that day you must worship him. You could miss out on Monday, Tuesday, Wednesday, Thursday, Friday, Saturday, but Sunday was a *must.* You must worship him by going to 7, 9 or 11 o'clock Mass. The penalty for disobeying was eternal hell… To miss this occasion was not only a mortal sin, but to come under the thunder and exposure of the dreaded head mistress. I am angry when I think of the millions of children who suffered in the same way, not in the last century or the Dark Ages, but in this century. This recollection in my case goes far, as close as 1915, and mental torture went on for years and years after that. The fear of hell's flames was ever constant.'

Her imagination went to work on every aspect of the incredible story, putting her in yet further fear of damnation: 'It was unthinkable that you should eat or drink for hours before God was placed on your tongue. From an early age my imagination went to work, I had a picture of thousands of nuns all over the world and all those bakeries turning out God by the billion. I knew by the thought that I was committing a mortal sin and would have to go to the priest and put up with a penalty imposed on me to get me out of Purgatory…'

She began having dreams of dropping through layers and layers of darkness, struggling and groping for something to latch on to. Night after night she would scream out in her sleep from the dess-bed in the front room, where she was sleeping at the time. When she awoke she had no doubt that she had been on the way to Hell.

A dess-bed was a common option in crowded conditions, it was a bed that folded up into a cupboard to maximise sleeping space, and one can imagine that Kate, sleeping next to her, might have been tempted to fold her away during this nightmare period.

In another dream Catherine saw herself at the top of a flight of stairs with Kate and a man with no face. Kate and this man would take her by her arms and legs and swing her to and fro, to and fro, out and over the stair well, eventually throwing her down the stairs. Rose did little to pacify the child by reassuring her that she would be all right so long as she woke up before reaching the bottom.

When Catherine spoke to me about the nightmares she experienced after receiving instruction, I thought she was exaggerating, and I couldn't believe that she took her Catholic instruction so literally. But she did. She believed that the fires of Hell were the blast furnaces that lit up the sky over Jarrow, the town that represented the western boundary of her world.

The depth of her acceptance even astounded some of her friends. She once discussed having bad thoughts

The painting of St Paul's Monastery, Jarrow, is by Joseph McIntyre.

The little church next to Simonside School, which Catherine attended from the age of four. It was there on one Maunday Thursday that she first became conscious of Jesus Christ, the man who was going to die for her the following day and who, if she prayed to him every night, would give her everything she wanted. And did she pray!

and the confessing of them with a Catholic girl friend from school, who was amazed that she shared her biggest secrets with the parish priest. 'By! you are daft, you know. You don't look it, but you are.' When she went on to tell Catherine that a priest had tried to kiss her mother when she was a young girl, Catherine was aghast and convinced that she must be lying.

Others had a good deal less difficulty in empathising with Catherine, however. Her cousin, Aunt Mary's

daughter, Teri, knew exactly what she was talking about, even though she received her instruction fifteen years later: 'It was a terrible time for Catholics. If the Church said, "Jump in the fire," we would have all jumped in the fire, regardless of whether it was right or wrong. We were frightened to death!'

The point is that Catherine's imagination was more real to her than the streets of East Jarrow, and it was to that that the missionaries had made their appeal. The alarming nature of their message is evident in such as Magdalen Goffin's *Objection to Roman Catholicism*, where the Catholic Catechism, drawn up by Cardinal Gaspari for children making their first Communion, says: 'In Hell, the devils, and with them the damned, are tormented with real fire and other most grievous pains.' An essay, called *A Night of Hell* describes a girl who, in her earthly life, had been inordinately fond of dress, as being condemned to wear forever burning flame: 'The blood was boiling in her veins, the brains were boiling in her skull, and the marrow in her bones.' In *The Teaching of the Catholic Church*, a certain Dr Arendzen tells his readers, 'If all that was ever written or painted or carved, expressive of the tortures of Hell, could be brought before us at a glance, it would certainly fall immeasurably short of the truth.'

Small wonder that doctors had to deal with children terrified out of their wits. With fear on most of their minds, the children of St Bede's Infants were ushered to St Paul's Jarrow *en masse* to confess. On Catherine's first occasion, instead of entering the penitent side of the confessional, she made the mistake of bursting in where the priest sits and getting tied up with his cassock and knees. Terrified, she was taken by the scruff of the neck and pushed into the eerie darkness of the other side, where she knelt alone and looked through a black grill at the outline of the Father Confessor, who, she would point out years later, had less similarity to a priest than to his chief antagonist from below.

In 1916, not long after the birthday party exclusion, Catherine moved from St Bede's to St Peter & Paul's school. The area was already known to her, close to the tram terminus and in the vicinity of the pawn and outside beer shops that she trawled for Kate.

Roman Catholicism had come to Tyne Dock more

The Tyne, 1879-1880, around the time that Roman Catholicism came to South Shields in the shape of Father Kirwan, and some years before the first mission was established in Tyne Dock.

recently than it found Jarrow. The Protestations of 1642 listed ten Catholics in Jarrow, none in South Shields and it was some 250 years before the first Catholic mission found a foothold, despite a huge increase in population in the interim. Perhaps the missionaries took their time because they followed Irish settlers, who chose to live in Jarrow rather than Shields, which is why the Geordie accent was always stronger there.

The first Catholic church appeared in Whitehead Street in 1873, sharing the Exchange Building with the Whitburn Coal Co, the Swedish Consul and a policeman. So great was the need, however, that the priest, a Father Kirwan, could drum up a congregation for three Masses a day.

Then, in 1884, the first Catholic mission was set up in Tyne Dock itself, and in the summer of 1889, a chapel and a school were dedicated to St Peter and St Paul on the north side of Bolden Lane. Finally, on September 23, 1905, the foundation stone was laid for a church there. It opened a year later, on July 6, a matter of weeks after Catherine was born.

St Peter & Paul's first incumbent was one Father Bradley, immortalised

The church of St Peter & St Paul, Tyne Dock, which lay at the centre of Catherine's world and opened just weeks after she was born.

as Father O'Malley in *Kate Hannigan, The Fifteen Streets, The Blind Miller* and *Colour Blind*. He had come from St Paul's Jarrow at the end of 1899, where he had served as curate. What was needed down the road in Tyne Dock was no ordinary priest – he had a parish to create and a church to build. Clearly, Bradley was the man for the job. To raise money he would stand against the dockers on pay day, as they flooded through the dock gates, shaming them into parting with their wages before they hit the pubs on the dock bank opposite. He even arranged for contributions from Catholic miners to be deducted from their wages at source.

Bradley was tough. As his builders would record, this man of God brooked no dissent. To the children of Tyne Dock he had a mesmeric effect.

Firing their imaginations with a primitive Old

Testament fear of Almighty God, he was the architect of their nightmares, but he also cared for his people. When in her teens he heard that Catherine was without work, he had a word with a town councillor, William MacAnany, who arranged employment for her in Harton Workhouse. That was typical.

'Father Bradley was all our lives until 1945,' recalls Winnie. He died on July 14, aged 75 (about the same time as Catherine was railing at the Catholic Church in the throes of mental breakdown). Years later, Winnie told me, 'Catherine paid for the heating to go in the church.'

I asked her what Bradley was really like. 'He wasn't the modern type of priest at all. He was a man apart, he lived in the Presbytery and *nobody* went near the Presbytery. (Nowadays the Presbytery is our parish rooms.) He looked very austere. But, Catherine *was* different from most people because she actually went to him and told him that she wanted to be a nun... I wouldn't have dreamed of approaching Father Bradley about that at all! She must have had that sort of *better outlook*.'

The fact was that both Catherine and Father Bradley were tough and singular people, and she dealt him many a body blow in the novels, as it fell clear that the stories he told were untrue.

In *The Blind Miller*, Sarah Bradley makes a clear distinction between religion and the interpretation put on it by the Catholic Church, and in particular by Father O'Malley. This became Catherine's ultimate position, and given that she is shooting an autobiographical line, it is interesting to note that Sarah was twelve years old before she could accept the fact that Hell was not the local blast furnace, and that even as a grown woman she could not shake off the belief that people paid for their sins in a hell that was administered by God.

Catherine tore into the Catholic Church in her autobiographical writings, as well as at length in interview with me. But like everything in her early life that she attacked most bitterly, it was forever a part of her, and during her teenage years it offered a much-needed balance.

There were moments when the great vacuum of aloneness that Catherine felt, took her so far down that it seemed to be echoed in everything around her. 'Do you know that for years I hated the sunshine because it showed up the greyness?' she once said to Tyne Tees Television. 'The greyness seeped in from outside, with the men with the grey clothes and the women with the everlasting pinnies and the stark gantries piercing the low sky…' It was a theme she would explore in *The Fifteen Streets*, where John Hetherington blames the sunlight not only for showing up his surroundings, but for hurting him deep inside.

The streets of Tyne Dock and East Jarrow were actually kept very clean in those days, so clean in fact that when, in years to come, Kate followed Catherine to the South, she would comment on how much more dirty were the streets there. There was, of course, more of a smog in the industry-intensive North, but the greyness refers as much to mood in the novel, a mood caused by the deep depression in the economy from the 1920s. For some time in Catherine's young life there had been more dark than light for other reasons, and for all its faults, the Church did much to succeed where the sunlight failed.

The Church succeeded by awakening Catherine to rare feelings of joy, though it was as rare for her to write about that in later years. In papers in the Boston University archive, she writes: 'I have known joy without knowing its cause. I was going up Hudson Street one day when I suddenly left the ground. I leapt from the ground up in the air. It was bigger than an ordinary jump and when I landed I said to myself why did I feel happy? I'd got nothing to feel happy about, because about this particular time [the word, possibly a name, is crossed out] had been on again, which meant that the money had been more plentiful and the drinks had been freer. But at different times in my youth I've had to deal with sudden bursts of joy which, if they did not lift me physically from the ground, sent my spirits soaring heavenwards. It never stayed long this feeling, but long enough for me to remember that it did actually happen.'

This state of ecstatic happiness she put down to the Virgin and the Holy Family. It was rare for her to walk by the church of St Peter & Paul's without dropping in. It would generally be in darkness, save for the light of the reserved sacrament, but she would grope her way down the main aisle and then into the Lady Chapel, where she would kneel before a statue of the Mother of Christ and share her feelings with Her.

First she would bless herself, then she would lift

Catherine would kneel in front of the statue of Our Lady and Holy Child that hung on a pillar at the front of the church, by the side altar on the right of the main aisle.

the Sacred Heart Medal that hung round her neck on a brass chain, and place it on her coat where it might be most visible to the deity. Then she would begin.

Generally any requests would be of a mundane nature. She would chat with the Holy Family rather like Don Camillo, the Italian priest in Giovanni Guareschi's series of books, who shares his everyday thoughts with God as if He were a very earthly friend. Catherine might ask the Virgin Mary to give her a hand stopping Kate's drinking or a hint as to who or where her father might be, or, almost as important at the time, she would ask Her to help keep her a good girl, her thoughts, words and deeds pure.

Catherine believed in God wholeheartedly as child and young woman, and Christianity would be revealed as a deceit second only to that of the dissemblance of her birth when she discovered that the stories were not true. She really *was* Mary Ann Shaughnessy in her novel, *A Grand Man*, whose requests to God are in similar vein: to have Him stop her da drinking and enable the whole family to move house (Mary Ann is convinced that a move to the country will do the trick).

What charmed so many about the eight-book series was the character's frankness, trust and innocent humour, and the Church gave Catherine the opportunity to exercise these qualities, which relieved her of the resentment and bitter aggression she exercised elsewhere. And even after the Church let her down, it left her with one precious gift, which she never forgot – a vision of a power untrammelled by the material world, a glimpse (so she believed) of what the love that eluded her actually is.

It happened in her early teens when she was finding her feet after leaving school and beginning to assert herself against Kate's demands in the beer and pawnshop department. She went with Olive Swinburn to visit friends of hers on Stanhope Road. Olive, a girl from the New Buildings, has the distinction of having brought to a sharp close Catherine's reign of terror by knocking her off her feet when she had uttered the words, 'Aa feel like a fight!' Now, Olive was about to make full recompense.

When they arrived at her friends' house, Catherine met a boy whose eyes were deep and dark and whose skin was creamy. She thinks of him as her first love, though it would appear that they never walked out. He was slim, he walked with grace, he was a beautiful lad, and Catherine used to hunt for Olive Swinburn in the hope that she would take her to Stanhope Road. His name was Hughie Axill.

One day she was walking from Tyne Dock towards East Jarrow through the famous arches when she espied him. He was with a pal, short and fat. As she walked towards him a feeling of utter joy swept over her. Then a strange light, a silver haze, seemed to suffuse the scene. She was convinced that she was not day-dreaming. Before she knew it she had passed them in this silver haze, and they were gone.

The image of it never left her, however, so that years later she would celebrate it in one of her very best novels, *Pure As The Lily*.

She gives the experience to Mary Walton, and the silver haze becomes uncreated light, a light that does not belong to the material world, a light signifying love, pure as the lily, for which Catherine so yearned.

5 Up By The Roots

'On the day in 1914 when war was declared, I recall flying down to the Slake bank, and there I sat looking across the mud flats waiting fir the war to begin. There was a pontoon in the river, but it never fired a shot.'

Grandma Rose died on December 13, 1917, the year after Catherine moved from St Bede's Infants in Jarrow to St Peter & Paul's School, Tyne Dock. In the wake of the loss of the only mother Catherine had known, she began writing her first stories. She was 11.

One year later, on September 5, just before the end of the First War, Uncle Jack was killed in action in France, which left just three living at No. 10 – John McMullen, Kate and Catherine.

Then, towards the end of the following year, 1919, Catherine had an accident in the playground at school and injured her leg at the hip. She remained off school until the following Spring, when she was formally withdrawn from St Peter & St Paul's, having attended only intermittently for less than three years.

I have never before told what I am about to say now. It was Christmas week. I must have been in my thirteenth year. It had been snowing during the week and on this particular day, Kate put into my hand a ten shilling note and a bass bag and told me to go to Tyne Dock and get three bottles of beer. I must have protested that my leg was hurting and her answer came back, 'You went out to play snowballs yesterday. Well, if you go out to play snowballs you can go a message so get yourself away.'

It is odd. She put the note into my hand. I cannot remember having a purse or a bag during my childhood or my early teens. I carried the money in my hand and brought the change back in my hand. When the pain was bad in my hip I limped, but at other times it didn't seem to trouble me so I can understand why she thought I was putting it on. That day she did not give me a halfpenny for a tram to Tyne Dock, because likely she hadn't another penny in the house. So I had to walk.

Now, at the bottom of the steep bank opposite the dock gates there always stood a paper boy. On this particular day I knew that I could not walk up that bank. My leg was aching terribly and I was trailing my foot. And what did I do? I went up to

The paper boy was poorly clad and it was a bitter day.

this boy and I asked him, would he go a message for me as I had a bad leg and couldn't walk up the bank. He said he would, so I placed in his hand the ten shilling note and the bass bag. What I went through as I waited for that boy to return were ages of eternity filled with terror, knowing what Kate would do to me when I managed to get back home and tell her what I had done. That boy returned with the three bottles of beer and the change, and I gave him a penny. I recall he was poorly clad and freezing with the cold because it was a bitter, bitter day, and although my situation was poor, the boy's was much worse.

I never told Kate of this episode because she would have gone mad to think that I had been such a fool as to trust a paper boy.

Over the years I have thought of that incident. A ten shilling note would have been a fortune to that child because he was only about 10 or 11 years old. He was cold and hungry and likely one of a large family, all in the same boat. All that I remember about him otherwise was that he kept hopping from one foot to the other.

This scene was painted for me by Catherine just a year before she died, a real-life episode, strands of which echo through the early novels which, as I have said, so often take off from this point in Tyne Dock. Her purpose was to impress upon me the honesty of the paper boy in the dire circumstances in which he lived – 'That incident has grown in my mind with the years,' she concluded. 'If miracles could be handed out to honesty then there was one.' But there is more to it than that.

Certainly it is worth dwelling for a moment on the fact that this was a truly terrible time for the Tyneside poor, as their plight worsened year on year until the General Strike of 1926. As Doris Johnson said to me, '1906 [the year of Catherine's birth] was as good as it got, it was downhill from there.' The strike was only ten days in May, but the number of people seeking 'relief' in the local workhouse soared from 13,366 to 36,768, a figure far from the highest. By the 1930s, 75% of insured men were out of work. 'We used to see the workhouse men when they exercised,' recalled Winnie,

Men waiting to be taken on outside the Shipping Offices at Tyne Dock. By the 1930s, 75% of insured men were out of work. In the New Buildings community people rallied round, but the poor house in Newcastle (below) was busy.

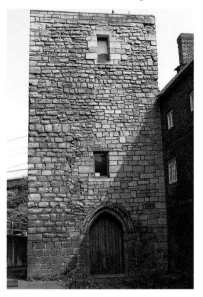

'they used to take them walking around the road, maybe to East Jarrow, such poor people.'

During this period, a woman might expect to work half days cleaning or washing and be paid two shillings; a half day was five hours. There were times when Kate would rise at 5 am, prepare the meals for the day – there might be three or four lodgers – start work at 8, turn out a house from top to bottom, and be back at 7 pm.

Yet it is Cousin Sarah's contention that Catherine exaggerated the hardship of her life: 'You know, Kitty talked about her abject poverty, if you look at her photographs as a child she's got ribbons in her hair, a lovely dress. Well, in those days kids who lived in poverty had no shoes on their feet. So there was a lot of untruth that Kitty told. There was sadness, a lot of lodgers, and family didn't go down very often to be honest, but…'

People do appear from the photographs of the period to look uniformly smarter than today, partly perhaps because most are dressed in similar attire. Also, Catherine's pretty clothes will presumably have been put on specially for the photographer, but Sarah's point has been made by others. The story of the

With poverty came queues for the soup kitchen at the Newcastle Poor House (above and right).

paper boy carries a visual sense of the wretchedness of life on the Tyne at the start of the third decade of the 20th century, but Catherine's limp insinuates her on the scene, centre stage, almost demanding our compassion. She seems to be incapable of telling a story, fact or fiction, without, in the process, unravelling something about her self and often calling on our sympathy.

The paper boy story immediately brought to mind a scene in *Colour Blind,* which features the orphan, Tony, who has one leg an inch shorter than the other. Not only has Tony no parents, as Catherine felt she had none, but he walks with a limp. Bridget, natural daughter of the Mcqueens, the family that has adopted him, is Tony's favourite person. By the fire at night Bridget would always sit next to Tony and make sure he was all right, and out in the street where other kids would make fun of his limp, calling after him, 'Hoppy on the Don,' she would walk beside him and, to make him feel better, sometimes deliberately pretend to have a limp, too

In real life, 'Hoppy on the Don' was the name given to a poor cripple who would sit on the bridge over the River Don, close to St Paul's Monastery. Kate had taken to applying it to Catherine. Had she, like Bridget, affected her limp?

Below, far left, Katie playing Hoppy, the cripple, who would sit on the bridge over the River Don (below).

Clearly, Kate suspected that she had, and Catherine had made the thought part of the novel. When I took her up on it, she became excited and insisted that she hadn't been shamming, still arguing her case forcefully sixty years on!

Given the extent to which she lived inside her imagination, it seems likely that she was not averse to courting compassion by affecting illness – we have already seen how envious she was of Mary, Aunt Sarah's daughter from Birtley, whose TB made her the centre of attention. If so, it appears to have tested Kate's tolerance at home, and at best, to have earned her only pity, compassion's poor relation – (she would write about the distinction between compassion and pity in *The Obsession,* in the context of Dr Falconer's relationship with Beatrice Steele).

Without question, in her early teens Catherine decided that other people's *envy* was better than their pity, and this period of her life, 1920 to 1929, is the story of how, with that in mind, she developed her extraordinary desire to succeed, an ambition as yet without a clear purpose or direction.

This change of tack from her aggressive and self-pitying stages was also the start of a healthy drive for freedom from the environment in which she had so tortured herself since the chimney-piece episode outside the Richardsons' house, and it would reach a pivotal point in 1929 with her leaving the North.

Couched, at the start, in her continuing determination to show the people of the New Buildings what she was made of, her ambition was encouraged by other factors, too, such as her feeling of apartness, which was endemic and which made her yearn for self-dependency without loneliness as its partner. There was also, as we will see, the negative influence of an upstart in the family, who spun her a tale about her father which made her more unpopular and so encouraged this loneliness. But whatever forces were brought to bear, this period was surely a progressive one. Unconsciously, she was working towards making the traumatic split with her mother a permanent one, which was the only way to go. Pulling herself up by the roots had to be the progressive option, and only then would Catherine begin to build a life.

Ambition gave her the momentum to break out of a shell of an existence in which she felt increasingly she had no place. But would it fill the vacuum left by the sadness, the lovelessness of her story to date, especially if cast, as it would be for a while, in this desire to be envied? Hers was a thoroughly modern strategy, and it was eventually fantastically successful materially, but would it succeed emotionally?

From her teens, all her relationships were linked in some way to her ambition, and they all failed. Contact on a more personal level, including sex, was shunned. Even the one friendship she made with a girl, Lily Maguire, was notable for Catherine pressing the Maguire family into helping her get on.

Catherine's relationships with boys were unimportant, except one with miner's son Mickey Moran, whom she allowed to give her presents, but only on the understanding that he would mount a search for her father, an integral part of her ambitious project. The one serious affair was with a man eleven years her senior, but he reminded her of the well-to-do man her father might have been, and was linked to her ambition as a passport to the status she was now determined to attain.

Catherine never went back to school after the hip injury, and in the Spring of 1920, when the School Board man came round, Kate burst into floods of tears at the kitchen table, listing her woes and ensuring that he would never bother them again.

Initially, Catherine went to work as a 'daily' at a house on Simonside Terrace, cleaning, cooking and washing for a family of five, called Sowerby. The job soon palled and was clearly inadequate to her purpose.

It was then that she began pen-painting. Cushions, tray-cloths, mantel borders were decorated with floral displays painted in oils from the nib of a pen, and then marketed through the club, a week-by-week purchase system. 'Now I was in business, I was an artist, and I felt very proud of myself!' she wrote. She made a go of it until the effort – she had to work long hours in painstaking fashion to earn very little – outweighed the thrill of independence and achievement, whereupon she took another job in service, which again soon palled, and it was at that point that Father Bradley intervened and arranged for her to be employed as Assistant Laundress at the workhouse in West Harton, just south of Tyne Dock.

None of this sounds very opportunistic, but the pen-painting business was enterprising for a girl of 14 on Tyneside at that time. It lasted some three years and at least she had the sense to give it up when it proved inefficient. This, in a first business venture, can be difficult to admit, and Catherine herself subsequently got tied up in a few white lies to avoid loss of face.

She writes in *Our Kate* that she became ill. Dr McHaffie was summoned, pronounced that she was suffering from anaemia and pointed to the cause as lead poisoning from the paints she was using, i.e. she was *made* to give up.

In the original manuscript, however, there is no mention of McHaffie's diagnosis. Just before she gives up, Kate tells her about workers at the Puddling Mills in Jarrow, where Rose had worked, lining their stomachs against the toxic effects of white lead with a daily milk or stout ration. There follows a row – perhaps Kate putting it into her head that her work might be injurious to her health was the last straw in an already draining occupation. At any rate, Catherine stomped off up to the Maguires and poured out her troubles to Lily. She then determined to make a big change in her life. Whereupon Mrs Maguire gave her a shilling to pay to an agent, who found Catherine a job as companion maid in Westoe Village.

Catherine had met Lily Maguire at the St Peter & Paul Youth Club. She had gone to socials before. May

An agency sent her to a house in well-appointed Westoe Village (above), which flanks South Shields as it spills into the North Sea. Catherine's position was 'companion-maid', which seemed to her to carry just a measure of respectability. This, as it turned out, was what her mistress had hoped, for the job itself was a grinding 15 hours a day, washing, cleaning, cooking and serving, and not a moment of companionship. When Catherine left, after only a fortnight, she discovered that she had been the sixth to do so in the space of a year.

Affleck ran 'half pound nights' in the Methodist Chapel Hall in Lord Nelson Street, which included games, one of which was called Winkie, a kind of Postman's Knock. In spite of her granda's religious bigotry it didn't seem to matter that they were Protestants that she had to kiss!

It may be safely assumed that these were pecks, not full-blown kisses, for by her own account she was a good girl and craved people's good opinion, even well into her teens associating opening her lips when she was kissed with having babies.

Winnie emphasised that all children were innocent, then, but Catherine was never a physical person as teenager or young woman, justifying it to herself by raising a natural concern never to go the way of Kate, though her avoidance of physical contact may also be seen as consistent with her inability to give of herself emotionally.

She was aware of this and explored it in the novel, *Maggie Rowan*, where Maggie is, like Catherine, illegitimate, and wonders whether her avoidance of sex and dislike of physical contact in general is some sort of moral retribution for her father's sin.

When I heard that Catherine may have had an extra-marital affair later in life with a certain Dr Mannie Anderson, I went to meet him to ask about her attitude towards sex.

59

When I accused him, Mannie laughed until tears spilled from his eyes: 'Even though she is obsessed with sex in her books, Catherine was very prudish,' he said, 'and always very proper in the confined quarters of the Mary Ann Shaughnessy [the boat on which they holidayed with their respective spouses]. I remember once we came together and by mistake I put my hand on her breast. There was instant recoil. Even when you entered in upon a warm, friendly hug, she would push you away. Bodily contact was not something that Catherine found easy.'

At the onset of puberty she did, however, begin to have dreams about flying, traditionally connected with sex: the dreams involved walking down to the bottom of William Black Street, standing with her back to a telegraph pole, shouting, 'Go!' and flying up to the wires and along them to the next pole, hovering there for a

Catherine as a teenager, around the time she played Winkie, a kind of Postman's Knock. It didn't seem to matter that they were Protestants she had to kiss!

while before descending to the ground.

Psychologists tend to agree that such dreams have a sexual significance, but it is worth noting that 'flying' dreams for one of Freud's patients indicated not rampant desire but a shunning of 'every sort of contamination involved by intercourse with human beings.' His patient's dream of suspension – 'which raised her feet above the ground and allowed her head to tower into the air' – fulfilled her desire to remain apart.

This 'fear of contamination' is attached to a theme of repulsion running right through Catherine's life – her disgust at the 'scavengers', who inserted their long shovels through a hole in the backlane wall beneath the wooden seat of the netty to clear the dry midden when she was sitting on it, is mentioned time and again, although others claim that the scavengers only came at night. It was second only to her repulsion at being made to insert her finger into old John's chickens to see whether they were about to lay, or hold a fowl while he cut its throat, or her revulsion at having to unbutton his sodden trousers when he came home too drunk to put himself to bed, or her abhorrence of the smell of urine in the Harton infirm wards... The list is endless and the episodes all find their way into the novels in her effort to dispel them, as do her abhorrence for smutty talk and raucous laughter, early repulsions at the sound of her grandparents having sex through the flimsy bedroom wall, of being interfered with by a lodger at No. 10, and watching with alarm a drunken man with two drunken women stagger out of the gents public toilet opposite the dock gates, mauling each other and laughing caustically.

All these things serve to characterise her recoil from the physicality of life on Tyneside, but also alert us to the barrier that she was building around herself, her dislike of physical human contact. Later she would recall that her first proper kiss had been an agony not enlarged upon for many years.

Through her teens Catherine grew out of a pudgy pubescent body to become as tall and graceful as a river reed, 'if rather flat, like a boy, immature still.' (as she described her fictional counterpart in *Tilly Trotter*).

Later, around 18, that deficiency would change in proportions that embarrassed her. Now, in her early teens, boys were attracted by her budding beauty, her skin complexion and her hair, which was waist-length and

Corstorphine Town (above), the Arab quarter of Shields. Catherine was sensitive to prejudices that were alive in her society, such as against the Arabs, because she ascribed her own unpopularity to prejudice against illegitimates.

luxuriant, with a sheen like that of starlings' feathers. (One thinks of Rosie's in *Colour Blind*, and Cathleen's in *Kate Hannigan's Girl*, though Cathleen's was shorter).

Before her first half pound night in the Lord Nelson Street Methodist Chapel, Catherine went on a shopping spree to South Shields secondhand shops and bought a pale blue voile dress for seven shillings and ninepence (40p today). It was too big for her, but could be held at the waist by a ribbon. John McMullen took one look at her and said, 'Home by nine!'

It seems to have been a big occasion by the standards of the Protestant church hall, certainly Catherine was very nervous and she couldn't get McMullen's warning out of her mind. She knew what the upshot would be if she came home a moment after nine. Still, she seems to have done well. She was walked home by flirtatious, exciting, adventurous Ralph Mudgerly. Very wisely she had him leave her at the end of William Black Street. McMullen had once gone berserk when Catherine had praised the work of the Salvation Army, and in his bigoted eyes, for a strong Catholic to be brought home by a Chapelite wasn't far removed from associating with an Arab in Corstorphine

Town. (Corstorphine Town was the Arab quarter in South Shields and appears in many of the early novels, notably *Colour Blind*.)

John McMullen had locked the front door and gone to bed. When she arrived at the front door of No. 10, Catherine was overcome by a terrible fear, but rose to the occasion, knocking her granda up and foxing him with her attitude, never for a second stopping talking – 'By, Da, it isn't half cold, have you left me any tea on the hob?...' From that day she had her own key and never abused the privilege.

The Roman Catholic St Peter & Paul socials were also Church-run affairs, but in a school room. More often than not there was a very good pianist in attendance, whom Catherine describes as a 'dizzie blonde' and only fifteen. This could well be Ethel Maud Atkinson, mentioned earlier, who helped Catherine learn to play. Her brother John told me, 'Ethel was fourteen when she taught Catherine. My other sister, two years younger, used to go up and turn the pages for her. Ethel was that good that she beat her piano teacher, Mrs Lee. The neighbours used to come into the backyard to listen.' There was also a netball team at the school room and on one occasion Catherine was *elected* Captain. Rising by means of a popular vote was a new experience for her. Then, one Saturday night, she met Lily Maguire.

Catherine's best friends were miners. In the mining community you had the heart of industrial Tyneside, 'The power of the pit was like witchcraft; it could embody a community of stubborn, bigoted men into a bond of brotherhood, a brotherhood that stood un-challenged, for no other industry in the world united men as did a pit.' D H Lawrence, son of a miner, believed that the physicality of life made them 'deeply alive instinctively. They avoided really the rational aspect of life. They preferred to take life instinctively and intuitively.' It was this intuitive response that Catherine later observed in her own mother and drew on in the novels to generate her mythology of the North.

Lift to the coalface, the overseer would ride down on the lift roof.

families,' Catherine told me, probably because she found them through Lily. In their homes she saw the family values that were missing from her own life – the warmth, the caring, the fun, the teasing, but especially the belonging. She wanted it, but such was her damaged nature, she couldn't embrace it, seeing no disloyalty in describing Lily's father as a tiny man, and wondering why so many fine women were married 'to squirts of pitmen.' On another occasion she told Lily that while she would doubtless marry a gentleman, Lily would never get beyond her own class.

This was so typical of Catherine, who felt for Lily and her family enough to write a whole novel about their qualities, but resisted their touching her deep inside.

Aunt Mary chose a different route in, appealing not to emotion, but to Catherine's ambition, and giving her the best reason yet to court other people's envy.

Aunt Mary had taken a shine to Catherine from when she was a very small child, prettying her up and delighting in so doing because she knew Kate would be peeved that she was improving her daughter in a way Kate couldn't afford. She gave Catherine her first doll, which she kept until she was nineteen. Again, she insisted that Catherine wear her own string of pearls to a children's party when they were still living at Leam Lane

Lily was her first (and only) 'best friend'. She lived in the South Shields area of White Leas, the daughter of a miner. In an early unpublished manuscript Catherine praises Lily's beautiful character, lovely eyes and husky voice. For a while they went everywhere together, often by bicycle to visit Lily's relatives in Windy Lane or Catherine's cousins in Birtley. She owed a lot to Lily and to her sister, also. For half a crown, Maisie Maguire hand-printed the entire 16,000-word text of a short story Catherine wrote, called 'On The Second Floor', in 1922. The story was flatly rejected by the *Shields Gazette*.

Lily's 'beautiful character' may be divined in Catherine's novel, *Pure As The Lily*, set in the years of the slump at the time they were friends. She needed her sweetness, and particularly the warmth of the Maguire family. Lily's home tumbled with love. Her parents, especially her father, welcomed Catherine with open arms, and Catherine, with no father of her own, loved to visit: 'In my teens, my friends were all from mining

– 'I remember Mary foolishly putting around my neck her string of pearls. That party had a sad ending because I snapped the pearls and got a good spanking.'

It is said that Catherine was 16 when she first asked her aunt what she knew about her natural father. 'I never called her Aunt. "Mary, what was my Da like?"' she wrote in the original text of *Our Kate*. 'She looked sharply at me for a moment and said, "Oh, well now, you're asking me something. Well, he was a toff, tall and good-looking. Wore a coat with an astrakan collar, I remember and always had black kid gloves and a walking stick, and spoke la-di-da."'

This is now as essential a part of Cookson mythology as what was said at the chimney-piece outside the Richardson's house when she was 7. In this first draft there is no mention of a silver-topped walking stick, and she actually crossed out the phrase, 'coat with an astrakan collar', which became the well-worn peg on which her father's gentlemanly appearance has hung since first publication of *Our Kate* in 1969. Instead, she substituted the rather less ornate 'black overcoat'.

Here, too, she tantalises us with the news that she did later find out who her father was by admitting that Mary's picture was almost totally inaccurate:

Catherine began working as Laundry Checker at the workhouse – the Harton Institute, above – on October 22, 1924. The job involved not only checking the laundry in and out, but also a degree of responsibility over a workforce mainly composed of inmates, and she took her duties very seriously indeed.

except for her father's name [Alexander Davies] the information that Mary had given her, she would learn years later from Kate, bore no resemblance to fact at all.

At the time, the impact of Mary's description was considerable. On the back of it she devised a strategy of self-improvement which, when she took up her position as Laundry Checker at the workhouse in 1924, made her about as unpopular as anyone could be, and it served to distance her from the New Buildings community too.

Catherine took refuge behind the picture of her father that Mary had drawn her. Behind it, with her eyes closed to reality, she constructed a world in which she felt she truly belonged, and began to train herself for the centre stage role she intended to take in it. Thanks to Mary, she *knew* that she was different, and she used this difference against her own people.

The effect was disastrous, Reny told me. 'When Catherine was being all hoity-toity the mothers used to say, "That's the lady coming."' She got a taste of what people thought when she took some serge to a woman to make up into a dress for her. It came back a mess, looking like something made for an inmate of the workhouse. Catherine took it back, but the woman wouldn't alter it and said she'd got what a hoity-toity deserved.

So what sort of person would feed Catherine such rubbish? Mary was unlike her two sisters, Kate and Sarah, both physically and in character. While they were plump and cuddly and warm of nature, she was thin and, as Catherine said to me, 'Although I'd like to bet there wasn't a house in those streets and in the terraces that would come up to my Aunt Mary's, she was envious of anyone getting on, above her family.' Nothing much good came out of Mary's stratagems, it seems, because so often they were conceived in bitterness.

It is impossible, from this distance, to judge how character forming Mary's longterm influence was on Catherine, whose psychological problems offered a field day to a skilful, class-conscious manipulator, but what served to mix up her emotions further was that a few months after Mary's 'revelation', Kate decided to marry one of her regular lodgers and drinking partners, the stoker David McDermott. She even told Catherine to go and arrange things at the Register Office in South Shields. Then, one Saturday morning [June 30, 1923], bowed down with shame and a feeling of betrayal that

Catherine at 19 in 1925. She made a present of the photograph to David McDermott, the stoker, one of Kate's lodgers, who two years earlier had become her stepfather.

she couldn't explain, Catherine went to their wedding.

Impressively, despite the shame and feeling of Kate's betrayal, she does not appear to have resented her new father, who was a quiet, good man and not violent. Among Catherine's personal effects in the Boston University archive there survives a birthday card written by her 'To my dear Dad'. I knew that she had had no quarrel with David, but I also knew how deeply the marriage had disturbed her. Yet she made a point of naming him as her Dad. She could easily have put 'David', but she put his feelings before hers.

Nevertheless, she claims that it was from the day of the wedding that she became determined to find her

The Crown Cinema on Hudson Street, Tyne Dock, as it is today. In Catherine's youth it was the one and only venue when 'walking out' with a boy.

father. Some time in 1924, the year in which Catherine began working as Laundry Checker at the workhouse, Harton Institution, she approached Mary for more clues about her father and Mary told her that she thought he belonged to a family of brokers, who at one time lived in Newcastle. Thinking she had a lead, Catherine pressed a boyfriend into action.

At the time, she was walking out with a fella called Mickey Moran, one of the lads who went to the church socials. 'Walking out' in those days meant going to the Crown Cinema on a Saturday night or for a walk after Benediction on Sunday. Mickey was a miner and also a bookie on the side, so he had more money than most. He was also very generous. Sometimes Catherine would return to Harton Workhouse with two pound boxes of Terry's chocolates, and if she was on duty next day there

might be flowers sent up from the main gate. Impressed by his streetwise savvy, a chip off Rory in *The Gambling Man*, Catherine struck a bargain. If he found out who her father was, she would marry him. One supposes that Mickey did his best, but in the end he had to admit defeat.

Catherine's job as Laundry Checker at the workhouse involved not only checking the laundry in and out, but also a degree of responsibility over a workforce mainly composed of inmates, and she took her duties very seriously. She earned only £30 a year and could have got the job if she had herself been an inmate, which, on account of her illegitimacy, she might well have been, but it provided her with board and lodging, which served to distance her from problems at home.

The workhouse was a grim place of firm discipline, charitable intent and terrible sorrow. Conditions were harsh, and there was a punitive ethos and inhumanity in some of the workhouse methods, in particular the rule of splitting up families – parents and children all labelled like criminals with numbers on their garments.

A year or so before she died, Catherine told me, 'Harton Institute in those days was not far removed from the Dickensian era. All about me were men standing in groups, thin men, lost men, men who sat on smouldering tips, picking cinders all night in order to fill a barrow to be pushed into Shields or Jarrow, hoping to sell the contents for a shilling. Men who had lost hope, families whom I had admitted into the workhouse when on part duty in the evening, the men to go to one side, the women to the other, the children to the nurses' home or nursery... Or an old couple separated by premature age knowing they'd have to spend the rest of their lives in the workhouse.'

The Minutes of the Guardians of the Workhouse do little to contradict Catherine's words. They are packed with despair, refusals of applications from families for the repatriation of their children, and so on. It was a strict regime.

On the other hand, before the advent of the welfare state, workhouses up and down the country performed a vital function, catering for the poor, for orphans, for illegitimates, the mentally and physically diseased and the old. Many thousands would not have survived without them, and Harton enjoyed a few notable successes,

Cleadon Cottage Homes in 1912. This is where children of families taken into the workhouse were sent. Children were separated from parents, husbands from wives. The agonies of the Receiving Home are constantly paraded in the workhouse records: an 8-year-old George Todd, separated from his parents, is not allowed out to live with his grandpa. A family of children called Matheson are kept in because their parents' house is not found good enough on inspection. There is a vote that no compensation should be made for a child called Emily who lost an eye due to poor workhouse administration because her travel costs to Sunderland Eye Infirmary had already been paid on her behalf. And so on…

where, for example, a child was supported through school and then further education into a professional job as a teacher.

In effect, working at Harton brought together the two strands of Catherine's life, her religion and her ambition. She may have stuck her nose in the air too much in the company of her fellow officers, but she brought it down to the level of the inmates, for her heart went out to them.

Feeling compassion surprised her, and she saw its propensity to heal. The men's casual ward was particularly bad and acknowledged as such in the Governors' Minutes. Men crowded in, sleeping on beds with blankets for bedding; when the boards were full they slept on the floor. Catherine describes in *Our Kate* the ward called Infirm 1, where the stench of urine stung her nose and where two ladies, both under thirty but looking twice that, sat in wheelchairs suffering quietly from acute arthritis.

At home at weekends, she would tell Kate and old John about them, and on a Sunday night she always brought them something cooked by Kate – scones, chutney, sometimes even a cooked chicken.

So, beneath the constant unforgiving pitch at which Catherine tended to operate, there was a more harmonious, human side emerging and best of all a sense of humour. The impression is of Kate and John pleased, even relieved, and they would eagerly anticipate her homecomings to hear some new story, perhaps about her deaf laundry helper, Mary Gunnabout, Catherine mimicking

In May 1925, the male casual ward was described as 'bad' by the Workhouse Master.

of the Kehedive's palace in Egypt were really derived from Smiles and not the *Koran* – 'You ought to know Smeelis! They are from his *Self-Help*; they are much better than the texts from the *Koran*!'

Smiles' guiding idea was that 'the most important results in daily life are to be obtained, not through the exercise of extraordinary powers, such as genius and intellect, but through the energetic use of simple means and ordinary qualities, with which nearly all human individuals have been more or less endowed.'

Above all, he attacked 'false gentility…superficial respectability…' and urged working class progress, despising 'an ambition to bring up boys as gentlemen or rather "genteel" men – the result is only to make them gents… The respectability that consists in merely keeping up appearances is not worth looking at in any sense.'

In this, Smiles helped Catherine to distance herself from the pretentious influence of Aunt Mary. He was one reason why Kate, in later years, could justifiably

Infirm I, the ward of the strong smells and two youngish women prematurely aged by pain, one looked like 70 – 'I think her name was Mrs Hannigan, I'm not quite sure… both were Catholics and, to my mind still, both saints.'

Mary to perfection on the subject of why she had left her last place in Shields. It was on account of a 'boot-chair boy' (a butcher-boy) who tried to lure her into the wash-house to give her 'a bit of meat'. She had her granda and Kate doubled up with mirth and for years old John would greet her with, 'Goo way boot-chair boy, goo way.'

Harton also gave her a taste of freedom away from the confines of No. 10 and the claustrophobia of the New Buildings, and to sharpen those qualities which she hoped would streamline her for success.

Here, in her off-duty hours, she groomed herself into a woman of culture – she studied the violin, French and anatomy (thinking perhaps that she might become a nurse). She also had a daily exercise regime, including martial arts, aimed at reducing weight and adding poise.

Among the books she read at this time was one called *Self-Help* by Samuel Smiles. This wasn't some tacky little manual. First published in 1859, it became a bestseller around the word. According to the famous historian, the late Asa Briggs, the book once prompted an Arab to remark that the mottoes written on the walls

The workhouse laundry. 'The checker whose position I filled,' Catherine told me, 'is the furthest left of the women wearing Sunday uniforms. The girls without caps are paid hands (see how happy they are?), the rest are inmates.'

wag her finger at the sometime children of the New Buildings who had despised Catherine, saying that her daughter was no upstart because hers had been an unpretentious, straight and honest bid for freedom.

Smiles failed to stop Catherine alienating some of her colleagues at the workhouse, however. Female staff would gather at the Refectory tables at lunchtime and crack dirty jokes or fool about apparently in louche fashion. This appalled Catherine, just as Kate's drunken antics had appalled her. She stood for it for as long as she could and then brandishing a bread knife, Miss McMullen, the youngest and rawest recruit (by this time known as 'Mac') loudly upbraided them. There was silence, before an older officer, called Morgans, who worked in the asylum block, brought the scene to ground by christening her 'bloody St Catherine' and telling her to sit down.

Catherine had set a seal on herself by her action and henceforth it would be open season on bloody St Catherine. For her part, she continued to put down much of the abuse she suffered to her illegitimacy, pointing out that there were eighteen members of staff in her department and it didn't take long for the word to get around. She had a point, since, as I have said, illegitimacy was a ticket into the workhouse as an inmate not as officer, and, again, although she wouldn't have seen it that way, her drive and overweening behaviour was sourced defensively in repressions sourced in her illegitimate birth.

The Harton experience did nevertheless gradually enable her to cope better with the antagonism that her damaged nature caused. She learned, in

Above, Catherine at 20 was convinced that being a child of passion marked her out as the lowest of the low.

that she finally took a large piece of paper and listed all the defects that the young woman had noted about her, adding words to the effect that a monster answering the description was loose in the workhouse grounds – anyone catching sight of it should alert the authorities! She then pinned the paper on the dining room mirror, where the notices went.

She had discovered the power of humour to take the sting out of a situation, and immediately it served her well once more.

Her self-improvement programme had begun to extend to the tendency rife in her family to mispronounce: 'How did one pronounce "subtle"? I had always heard it spoken as "subtill". How was one to know?' she wrote. In her room she began to articulate words loudly, and once, when the bell rang and she dashed out of the door to meet an appointment, she caught a huddle of inmates giggling at her keyhole. But at least now she could 'laugh with those who laughed at me.'

With some of her skills training, however, she was finding less success. Her French teacher soon gave up on removing the Geordie in her accent, and Catherine proved so inept at the violin that Matron's dog would immediately start howling, which really only reflected every one else's opinion.

What knocked her back especially were rejections that she could not attach to prejudices about her background – to her illegitimacy or the kind of family she came from. If she could name these to blame she could move forward with firmer resolve. But when she sent a

particular, how to avoid or de-fuse conflict rather than look for it, and in difficult circumstances.

One day, when making use of some Indian clubs in her fitness programme, colleagues hid, giggling at what they saw. Pretending not to have heard them, she approached their hiding place whirling the clubs and dancing a slow waltz and singing a tune before tipping the lot over them and making a slapstick joke of it.

When her room-mate stole a present to Catherine, a box of soaps, and suggested that flowers dropped off by Mickey Moran were in exchange for sexual favours, she was furious, but stopped herself hitting the girl 'by remembering to say the name of Our Lady.'

The same person so assailed Catherine with abuse

The Ravensworth Arms at Lamesley, where Kate had lived and worked, met Catherine's father and conceived her.

Below: St Peter & Paul Church, Tyne Dock, where Catherine first met Jim Dailey, a man eleven years older than her with whom, for the first time in her life, she fell in love.

Right: the little street where they first kissed. Catherine had been born opposite, next to the Alexandra pub: 'We had taken shelter, of all places, round the corner of this little street where I had been born, next to a public house. And as he stood waiting for a tram he bent and kissed me. I was down with wonder.'

play she had written about a workhouse to a writer's correspondence school, and they wrote back: 'Strongly advise author not to take up writing as a career,' she was absolutely devastated. Worse, the rejection coincided with a particularly difficult time she was having in a relationship with a man eleven years older than her.

Catherine had first noticed Jim Dailey in the congregation St Peter & Paul's when she was 15: 'I longed that such a man could be my father because that was the beginning of a period when I began secretly to search for him.'

Dailey was a professional man, in insurance. Winnie remembers him as 'very dignified. I knew of the family, not him, they were beyond me.' One day in 1925, when Catherine was 19, he walked her home after Mass. For two years they would go to Mass and the Saturday pictures, but strangely he always declined Catherine's invitations to dances, and she was convinced that her workhouse persecutors revelled in the misery this caused her.

Dailey didn't kiss her for a year, but when he did she was 'down with wonder… It was gone night. It was sleeting badly. We had taken shelter. He was waiting with me for the Jarrow tram. We had taken shelter, of all places, round the corner of this little street where I had been born, next to a public house. (Oh, I had to be born next to a public house! And within ten yards of the actual Dock wall.) And as he stood waiting for a tram he bent and kissed me.'

Catherine believed she was in love. This was a huge development in her loveless life. 'And then he told me why he had been so reticent. He had been getting over a love affair. He had discovered just before he was about to marry, that his future wife was subject to epileptic fits. I could see now, I had been used as a source – I was kind, I was sympathetic…'

Catherine could have borne this if Dailey had then played a proper part in her life and accepted invitations to dances and functions associated with her work. But he did not. 'Not once during the following year did he ever deem to accompany me to a public place. The excuses were many and of all kinds. And what I suffered from the main part of the staff was unimaginable… How many nights I cried my eyes out, asking the question why? Why?'

Then, somehow – whether it was Catherine's doing or Dailey's is not clear – plans were laid for a holiday in Cumbria. To preserve appearances, she was to go on ahead. Catherine had never been so far away before and excitedly made friends with other tourists before he arrived. She was on form and proved very popular in the pub where they stayed, but her performance made Dailey feel almost superfluous. Now no longer in the

On holiday in Cumbria Catherine shone and, once out of the suffocating environs of Tyne Dock, came alive, taking the lead away from Dailey in their relationship.

driving seat of their relationship, he became possessive and had his nose really put out of joint when Catherine accepted an invitation to travel to Scotland, with Dailey tagging on morosely behind.

Back home Catherine's workhouse colleagues assumed that the holiday had gone rather better than in fact it had. A 'violet ray installation' had been purchased to treat, state the Workhouse Minutes, diseases like 'rickets, malnutrition, surgical tuberculosis and tubercular glands…also lupus,' and staff were offered a free course. As Catherine sat awaiting her turn, dressed only in bra and knickers, a superior noticed a spot on her waist and had her subjected to a rigorous examination during which a doctor's free-ranging hands made certain confirmation that her hymen was still intact. At a time when sexual disease was rife, her holiday with Dailey had led to suspicions that she may have contracted syphilis. Apparently nothing could have been further from the truth.

Then, on June 20th 1927, Aunt Mary threw a 21st birthday party for Catherine:

Kate couldn't give me a party in our kitchen. But my Aunt Mary at the top of the street had made her three rooms into a very nice, comfortable home and her front room was well furnished. It even had a spinet piano in it. I invited eight of my associates, four of them real friends, they all brought their boyfriends. Mary had a very nice tea set out and we waited – and we waited – and we waited – and the main guest never turned up. Oh there was some laughter and gossip. Well, the next week a letter said he was sorry, but had been taking the money to pay an insurance claim and had lost it and he was very upset. He thought our friendship should stop because he would have to save up to repay the money that had been lost… My eyes had been opening slowly, and I realised the character of this 'gentleman' with a beautiful face marred by a very small mouth. [Only Catherine could have managed the put-down in interview with me more than seventy years on!] Coming to my real self at last I wrote him a letter that should have burnt his fingers as he held it.

Catherine then took off on holiday to Ireland, staying with McDermott's sister, who was stone blind. Belfast was bleak and the attentions of one Irish man in particular made it bleaker. She was assaulted, she claimed, on the top deck of a bus. It was then that she received a letter from Dailey, forwarded by Kate. 'It was to say that he had been to a priest and told him that he had made use of me over the past two years, not sexually, oh no, but as a salve to ease his hurt feelings. And the priest had said that he had done me a great wrong and he had to ask my forgiveness. After I read the letter I took up one sheet of paper and wrote across it three words - I wrote not in a straight line, but right across the page three words, "Go to Hell!" I did not see him for many months after.'

The bust up hit Catherine hard, but at the tail end of 1927 she was accepted for the vacant post of Assistant Laundress at Harton and her spirits rose, until one day she met Dailey coming out of the Crown Cinema.

He begged me to become friends with him again because he missed me so much. I laughed in his face. But he kept on and I lost the last bus home. There was only now what they called the drunk bus from Shields market to Jarrow. This was always full of men who had just come off the ferry. The pubs in Shields closed a half an hour earlier than those in North Shields, and the men, still able to stand on their feet, got on the ferry, went over the river for a last drink, came back and got on the bus. And it was into this bus that I had to be pulled by them onto the platform with my late suitor still begging me to write to him. The bus started and he walked along with it for a while and there I stood with those drunken arms around me, looking down at him, the man who had rejected me. And I felt in a way that I had won, but only in a way.

The drunks were very merry and they kept shouting to each other, 'She's not going to write to the lad!' And different voices, 'Why isn't she going to write to the lad?' 'The poor fellow's bad!'

'The poor fellow's sick!'

The bus stopped at the bottom of William Black Street. I got off to the cries of the merry drunks saying, 'You be a good lass and write to the fella. Now go on now.' I walked up the dark street to the house that had always been my home and as I did so, the smile left my face and from deep within me there came a cry and it said, 'I'll show him! I'll show him!' Of course I knew that I had been rejected not only for myself but because I was illegitimate. I came from a notorious family. It wouldn't do him any good in the insurance business to be linked up with such people.

Once again, she was at pains to explain her rejection in terms of her illegitimacy.

That was the end of my courting days so to speak. The fellow from the mental block began to ask me out. This caused a different kind of furore in the house. The staff came back to me in a hoard. Didn't I know he was engaged to be married? No, I didn't. So the next time he asked me I put the question to him. No of course he wasn't. Not any more. He had once been engaged to this girl but that was broken off ages ago. One Sunday dinner I was home for the weekend and was drying up the dishes with Kate in the scullery and there was a knock at the door. It was my dancing partner. He had come, he had actually come to ask me to marry him, with a special licence. I laughed. He was the last person on God's earth I would have married. The most intelligent part about him was his feet. When I went back into the scullery and told Kate we leant together for a moment. It was a rare moment. We laughed again. And then I went back into the front room and he asked me if I would write a letter for him. He wanted to get into the Halifax police. I did this for him and he went away very disappointed. A week passed and then the staff were in their glory, most of them, with the exception of my few friends were in their glory! My boss even came to me and

slapped down on to my desk a newspaper cutting. It was to say that a wedding had taken place on Saturday last and that his wife had given birth on the Sunday. I couldn't believe it. But it was true. And the staff had the time of their lives.'

The Tyne ferry, an image that Catherine carried in her mind's eye until the day, forty-seven years later, that she returned to live in Newcastle with her husband, when she made a point of taking a ride on it.

It is a telling mark of Catherine's emotional life that five of the men she courted in her twenties were married or heavily involved with somebody else. Whether her independent spirit gave married men the feeling that commitment was not an issue, or that, in the absence of a father, she was looking for the protection and security more likely to be found in a mature married man, is uncertain. But the deception involved in all these relationships served to re-affirm her mistrust in love and was food to the very roots of her psychological problems.

In January, 1928, Catherine applied for the newly vacant post of Laundress at Harton, and was turned down. In the wake of this rejection, and still smarting from the business with Dailey, she answered an advertisement in the *Poor Law Journal* and was accepted for the position of Laundress at Tendring Workhouse near Clacton-on-Sea in Essex.

So it was that in March, 1929, she made her momentous decision – with 'deviant exultation!' – to leave the North, determined to make something of herself and show them all what she was made of.

6 BREAK OUT

Tendring Workhouse, Essex, was built in imposing style in 1835.

On the day that she left, John McMullen walked her to the tram, the tears running down his stubble, for he only shaved about once a week, and somehow both he and Catherine knew that it was the last time they would see one another. She was one of a very few that felt anything other than fear or loathing for John McMullen, and at this moment what she felt was an overwhelming love for him. For was he not the only da she had known? Had not he alone, since the death of Rose, treated Catherine with respect and kindness and love, three qualities that he reserved for nobody else? As he pressed his white moustache to her cheek and said, 'Mind how you go,' she must have softened for a moment, before straightening up and turning to go.

Catherine took up the position at Tendring Workhouse in May 1929. It is as well to pause and consider what she had done. Like a nut from a shell she had broken out of her world of things and emotional entanglements, convinced that she had no place in them. Uprooting from a town, a county, a region was unusual in those days, and will have taken courage, particularly for a young woman from the North East, where ties are traditionally strongest. But in her case ties were not strong, she had reached this point in her life courageously, but in response to unrelenting negativity.

However true that she had rejected her own people, she, too, had been rejected, and this cannot have done much for her level of confidence beneath the bravado. She may have derived some comfort from turning down Dailey when he asked to come back to her, but her failure to win the position of Laundress, which followed the rejection of her play by the writers school, must have stung.

She did not blame her illegitimacy for not getting the job of Head Laundress, which is odd since she blamed it for her unpopularity there, and it is arguable that the social stigma wouldn't have recommended her to such a position of authority over the illegitimate inmates at Harton.

Instead, she came to the conclusion that Harton had rejected her because Matron feared the consequences of giving such a strong personality as hers the reins of power, and later she weighed this argument in the novel *Maggie Rowan*, where Maggie is given only a measure of responsibility in Mrs Thornton's laundry for the same reason.

Maggie Rowan is an efficient, difficult woman, bitter and repressed. Mrs Thornton is a businesswoman and sees her as the perfect assistant manageress in her laundry, but no manager.

Why? Because she sees that Maggie's control over her workforce is devoid of feeling and dependent on their dislike and fear of her. Thornton has no problem with this. She has noticed that it makes for an honest and highly efficient regime. Also, Maggie is unlucky with men, so there is little prospect of her getting married And yet, Thornton is absolutely clear about one thing, on no account must Maggie be given a position of supreme power – she must never be made Head Laundress – for 'once Maggie felt power she would be like the beggar on horseback…she'd ride to hell.'

Although Maggie Rowan is but a fictional aspect of Catherine, the significant point is that her creator accepts that there is something missing, a fault in the bedrock, which, in the novel is to do with bitterness, hate and lack of love – circumstances that favour ruthlessness and even cruelty, once in a position of control.

If her Harton matron did also think this, future events would not prove her wrong. Catherine threw her-self into her first managerial job at Tendring. The Master and Matron applauded her efforts, but before long her inexperience began to show. Most of the workers under her were older and resented the way she hurled her authority at them in an effort to galvanise everyone into a similar work rate to hers. Just as bad, Tendring itself was as quiet as a morgue, and this 23-year-old, who had

only twice before spent time away from home, began to fall back into feelings of loneliness.

The Tendring Peninsula supports an oyster industry and three resorts, Clacton, Frinton and Walton. Tendring village is five miles inland. The workhouse was built in 1835 in the midst of thousands of acres of farmland, facing west down a long, tree-lined drive to a road. Visitors were met by a single-storey entrance block, beyond which lay a courtyard and the wings of a large, three-storey building, the hub of the site. The peace of the place nearly drove Catherine mad, after living in busy East Jarrow, where the horns of ships, the rattle of trains and the whine of the saw mill lay constantly on the wind.

Clacton-on-Sea, the nearest town, is ten miles away. One Sunday morning she took a bus to Mass at the Lady of Light Roman Catholic church in Caernarvon Road, and afterwards asked the priest for an entré to a Catholic family. He told her that she would find plenty of people to meet in the town. By the time she caught the bus back late that afternoon, she had met no-one and was exhausted, lonely and very angry.

On a subsequent Saturday she travelled again into Clacton and sat sadly on the beach, looking out to sea. Suddenly her nose began to bleed. This nosebleeding had become a tiresome, regular event, first experienced when she was 18. She had devised various ways to stem the flow and now applied them, but the bleeding was unusually free and nothing could stop it, so she went in search of a chemist.

Concerned passers-by offered her hankies to sop up the blood, one a scarf even. By the time she found a chemist, she was desperate; the flow was, if anything, getting worse. She was given some wadding and told she must see a doctor. Off she set to find a doctor. Then, all of a sudden, she came to a stop with an odd sensation in her head: 'The only way I can describe it is as if some-one was pulling a sausage out of its skin.' She felt the blood clot moving across the vein in her head and falling 'like a thick rope' onto the wadding. Mercifully, the bleeding then stopped.

Her nosebleeds were always worse when she was under pressure, and Catherine realised she had to do something to brighten her life in Tendring. She decided to invite a friend down from the North and contacted

*Catherine in a field near the work-
house with her friend, Elsie
Chisholm, a hairdresser from
North Shields whom she'd first met
during the holiday with Jim Dailey
in Cumbria.*

Elsie Chisholm, a hairdresser from North Shields whom she'd first met during
the holiday with Jim Dailey in Cumbria. Elsie agreed to come and they spent
happy times together that first summer of her independence, but it was only
ever a holiday and soon came to an end.

Perhaps the Matron realised that Catherine was not settling well, for
when a vacancy for a job came up, she asked whether there were any more
hardworking girls like her up North, and Catherine began to hatch a plan to
import someone on a more permanent basis.

The person she chose to contact – one Annie Joyce, a former colleague at
Harton – was not in fact a particular friend, but Annie had once expressed a
desire to take a job away from home. Soon after she arrived, Catherine realised
what a mistake she had made. Annie was not on her wavelength, but more to
the point, she brought with her into Catherine's new, independent environment
a direct line into her past, and some of those who resented Catherine's position
over them now made it their business to use Annie to dig for some dirt.

Then, one evening when out walking, Catherine came upon a woman in
the garden of a cottage; her son was playing nearby. She spoke to the boy, who
commented on her North Country accent. One thing led to another and the
boy's mother invited the stranger into their home, where she met the woman's
husband. Later, Catherine observed that the couple were clearly at odds with
one another, 'at opposite poles.' She was rather parochial, he had an interesting
mind with no-one on whom to exercise it. As a result, he treated his wife badly.

Catherine was invited to return, and clearly buoyed by this man's con-
versation, she began to raise her act to him, he responded and his wife was
increasingly excluded. The climax to this difficult situation, to which Catherine
was anaesthetised more by her loneliness and need to be well thought of by

The photograph is hand captioned, 'Kitty, 1929', and clearly it is one of a batch taken during her first year of freedom from Tyneside when she persuaded Elsie Chisholm to come down from North Shields and cheer her up. Shortly, Catherine would embark upon an 'affair' with a married man that brought her to her wits end with shame and led quickly to her leaving the area.

someone than any desire for the man, came when, one afternoon, all four went to the Odeon cinema in Clacton.

Catherine sat next to the man and, as usual, they became preoccupied with each other, while the boy watched the film and his mother quietly fumed. Mid-way through the programme, the little boy asked to go to the lavatory and his mother asked her husband to take him. He refused. She, smouldering with fury, had no alternative but to take him herself.

When mother and son emerged from the Ladies, they pointedly sat some way away. In the car going home there was a terrible row and when finally Catherine was dropped off at the bottom of the drive leading up to the work-house, she did what she had always done when shamed – (as when she stole a comic from the local newsagent as a child, or watched as Kate stole a length of flannelette from a shop) – she vomited on the ground.

Once again having no-one else to blame, she had to face her guilt alone, and it hurt. She had come between man and wife, and the pain that the row will have caused their young son was by any standard of morality inexcusable.

Back in the day-to-day traffic of the workhouse, a way to close the door on her conscience did appear, albeit in rather an ironical shape. Annie had given in to the pressure of those trying to find a way to get back at their iras-cible manager. She had told them of Miss McMullen's secret.

In papers at the Boston University archive, Catherine records that when Matron was told of her illegitimacy, she was not happy. There was a row, which led to Catherine looking for employment elsewhere. Whether the revelation was in fact sufficient to bring matters to such a head, or whether it merely served her purposes to record it as such, cannot be said for sure. All that can is that Catherine began to make preparations for another clean break, and leave her conscience behind her.

In December, 1929, just eight months after she had arrived in Tendring, she answered another advertisement in the *Poor Law Journal*, this time for

Head Laundress at a workhouse in Hastings, Sussex. A letter came back giving a date for interview. Catherine, by this time, was desperate to get out of Tendring, and put her mind to how best to ensure that she got the job. There were three others in the running – a shortlist of four, and she was worried what Matron would say to the Hastings people when asked for a reference. She selected her clothes carefully, paying particular attention to her coat and choosing a Henry Heath hat to complete the picture.

On the 19th she travelled by train to the south coast resort and was shown around the workhouse with the other interviewees by Matron Silverlock, who was married to the workhouse Master. Catherine was then interviewed by the Board of Guardians. By now she could draw on five years experience and speak knowledgeably about the workings of a workhouse laundry. Moreover, what she had seen on the tour left plenty of space for improvement. So, she lost no time in giving the Board not only her opinion but also a list of things that could be done to put things right.

The strategy worked. Even after the Tendring matron wrote that she

thought Catherine too young, she got the job and on February 3, 1930, started work, finding lodgings in Clifton Road on the east side of town, around the corner from Cookson Gardens. Her weekly wage was three pounds, six shillings, much more than she would have been paid as Head Laundress at Harton.

Throwing herself into work, she set in motion a project to pave a sorting area in order to minimise the spread of dirt in the laundry; she instituted an efficient regime for her staff and began to campaign for better conditions for inmates – large grass plots were provided for the older inmates to enjoy picnics in pleasant surroundings, and Catherine organised these herself.

When the Portress fell ill, she volunteered to take over her duties in addition to her own and moved into quarters in the workhouse Lodge as a resident officer. Later, she also acted as Assistant Matron. In short, Catherine put herself out. She knew that this time she had to make it work, and so busy did she become that mention was made and recorded in the minutes of 'the frequent allocation of Miss McMullen as a Relief Officer,' and it was accepted that 'Miss McMullen is the only Officer capable of carrying out [the] work.'

She was nothing if not efficient and expected the same commitment from her staff. She was known among her staff as a slave driver and by some of them as something much worse. But this time Catherine did her best to win round both the other officers and the inmates, one of which proved very difficult. An asylum case called Jessie came at her with an iron bar used for lifting the door off the coke-heated flat iron stove. 'I called to some of the women to get her

The Hastings Workhouse was run until 1930 by the Guardians of the Poor – the Hastings Board of Guardians – after which the local Corporation took over the management. It remained a public assistance institution catering for the aged, infirm and destitute and a municipal hospital until 1948, when the NHS turned it into St Helen's Hospital.

It was nothing like as sad as Harton, however. Here the workhouse inmates could be considered to be on a picnic compared to those in South Shields. Catherine couldn't believe the treats and attention they got.

Catherine was the source of Matron's report on April 9, 1931, on 'the cramped out-door spaces allotted to the women for recreation. Could something be done to make it possible for the old ladies to enjoy the sun and air during the summer weather? At present they are obliged to stay in their respective wards most of the day... Large grass plots should be provided for them in pleasant surroundings.' Catherine organised the picnics herself.

from behind, but for once they turned a deaf ear to an excuse to stop work, and those who could disappeared into the sorting room.' Catherine managed gently to talk the woman down, backing her towards the stove, and when she was inches from it, suddenly threatened to push her onto it if she didn't hand the bar over. Fortunately Jessie dropped the bar, allowed herself to be led meekly away by the hand, and subsequently became as closely attached to Catherine as her shadow.

Then, on April 18, just two months after she had arrived, John McMullen died and Catherine was overcome with grief. She did not venture home for the funeral, however. Her beloved granda was, after all, gone, and with her own independence still far from established, she felt intuitively that it would not be advisable. Instead, she sent Kate £20 to cover the funeral expenses, learning later from Aunt Mary that only half the burial bill had been payed, and Kate had been rotten with drink.

McMullen's passing took the wind out of her sails and the endless hours of hard work and absence of any real friends began to depress her with the old feelings of loneliness and emptiness. For the first time since her arrival, Catherine took stock.

She was now a self-sufficient woman in charge of a laundry on a very decent salary. The three pounds and six shillings a week went a long way in 1930, when the dole was £1 – thirty shillings for man, woman and child – best butter was a shilling a pound, bacon threepence for flank, fourpence halfpenny for side, fivepence or sixpence for ham; 2 dozen eggs (small) were a shilling; margarine fourpence; and one pound of steak and rabbit was a shilling.

As Catherine recalled for the *Sunday Telegraph Magazine* in July of 1988, she was also rather taken with the town: 'Hastings was another world, in which everything moved at an easy-going pace and no one looked poor or even

drab.' It was here that she first encountered the middle-classes. A woman took her under her wing and gave her a tour of the area, referring to the *women* of Hastings Old Town and the *ladies* of St Leonards (an extension of Hastings, west along the coast). The distinction would inform the social character of Fellburn, the fictitious town in which so many of Catherine's novels are set, with Brampton Hill being St Leonards, where the middle-class ladies lived, and Bog's End deriving its class order from working-class Hastings Old Town.

There is some disagreement as to the extent of the impact of Hastings on the novels. I was told by a townswoman that she based the hero of *Rooney* on a local dustman, but Catherine herself told me that he was based on a dustman from Eldon Street, Shields. Feelings and places, such as Fairlight Glen in *The Man Who Cried*, discussed below, are certainly present, and characters do appear, such as Aunt Lot in *The Menagerie* – 'a poor young woman who is slightly off balance,' as Catherine described her to me. She came upon Aunt Lot in real life when she was walking along the sea front. She saw her standing by the old war memorial (now dismantled, much to the fury of Hastings townsfolk):

Looking out over Hastings Old Town towards the pier (right). The social stratum of the Old Town area became that of Bog's End in Catherine's fictional Fellburn, where so many of her novels are set.

Centuries before Catherine arrived, fishing was the main industry. In the mid-17th century 239 out of 280 heads of Hastings households were involved in it. However, from the 1830s, with the end of the smuggling boom, the south coast fishermen was seen off by competition from French boats, and at the same time, seaside towns became fashionable holiday resorts. With the coming of tourism, Hastings developed west along the sea front and joined up with St Leonards. Mr Parker's enthusiasm for the new recreational idea of a seaside resort in Jane Austen's unfinished novel, Sanditon, *is believed to have been influenced by the extension of Hastings into St Leonards. Catherine would try her hand at setting a novel in the town, too, but after six months concluded that there were more guts in the fish.*

She had on a voile dress, a pair of stockings that were wrinkled round her legs, high heel shoes that were over at the sides and made her walk in an odd way. But on her shoulders was a worn-out feather cape and on her head one of the old-fashioned, flower bedecked hats which were in fashion at the beginning of the century. I never saw her face. I only saw the back of her figure, and I remember the name that came into my mind from nowhere, 'Poor Aunt Lot.' Why I should think that name, I don't know, but she remained in my mind for some time. Who was she? Where was she from? Why dressed like that? She *was* an oddity. Now it must have been years later when I wrote *The Menagerie* that there she was all ready for me, straw hat, mouldy cape, summer dress and wobbly high heels.

All this was to come. What she liked immediately about Hastings was what Jane Austen recommended through the fictional Mr Parker in her novel, *Sanditon* – 'the finest, purest sea breeze on the coast'. And, as Catherine's cousin, Teri, pointed out, 'The south was always more genteel. The poverty was still there, but you didn't exactly see it the way it was up North.'

However, despite the gentility and the gusts of pure sea breeze, feelings of loneliness and negative thoughts continued to assail her in her most private moments. One weekend her landlady was away and there was no-one else in the house. Catherine went to the cinema to see *Bulldog Drummond*. In the middle of the film she felt loneliness descend upon her like a pall, and when she came out she fought back the tears until getting home, where she flung herself

on the bed and wept. The emotion brought on a nosebleed so strong that the thought came to her that she might bleed to death, *and why not?* It was the first time she had asked herself the question, but it would not be the last.

Soon afterwards there was a workhouse dance for staff, and Catherine made herself go. She was escorted by Master and Matron Silverlock, who were her only friends. A smart young man came over to their table – 'We'll call him Keith,' Catherine recorded. Keith introduced himself and asked her to dance. Then, mistaking the Silverlocks for her parents, he asked them if he might take her out. Catherine put him right, but agreed to go out with him.

The 'friendship', as she described their relationship, would last six months. Evenings out were spent mostly at concerts at the White Rock Pavilion. Keith was very fond of music. Catherine came to the conclusion that she wasn't at all musically minded, which wasn't in fact true, perhaps more of a comment on the concert programme, with which she went along because she liked Keith, enjoyed his company. He was interesting, a writer who had what she longed to have, a published short story. At the time, he appeared brilliant,

Seaside resorts out of season have a way of seeking out the loneliness in a person, and Hastings was no exception in the early months of 1930.

Catherine wrote of her aloneness as a separate character that was fast developing its own desolate life, into which it was sucking her, mocking her striving.

and yet, as far as affection went, Catherine could give him none.

This wasn't Keith's fault. By now, her hang-ups about men and sex had reached disaster proportions. It was as if she was inured against feeling, when it came to men.

Soon, however, Keith would give Catherine a reason to sharpen her feelings towards him.

Fairlight Cove lies on the coast between Hastings and Rye. It is a place of great beauty. Here, Catherine would love to walk, and later she rode a stallion along the cliff-top out of stables close to Rye, once daring to go bareback and falling into a trough of silage as she threw the wrong leg over his back to dismount. It was not this that soiled her longterm memories of the place, however, but another incident, not altogether inconsistent with being thrown by a stallion, as she showed years later when she wrote *The Man Who Cried*.

The novel marks out Fairlight Glen *(sic)* as 'a cursed place' – a place of infidelity and deceit. The demented Lena Mason follows her husband, Abel, to a rendezvous there with his lover, Alice Lovina, the very place where, in 1932,

Left: The glorious cliff-top walk from Hastings through Fairlight Cove (Catherine calls it a glen) to Winchelsea and Rye. It was chosen to establish the deception and violent emotions that motivate the novel because here Catherine's boyfriend, Keith, told her that he was married, and she very nearly pushed him over the cliff.

It is also the cliff-top path to Fairlight, where Catherine would ride her stallion bare back, and in The Man Who Cried, *Abel and Dick run through fields and over styles, right along the cliff top, in order to avoid the demented Lena Mason.*

Below: the cliffs at Winchelsea.

the unfortunate Keith dared tell Catherine that he had been deceiving her, that he was married, that he had that very day been to see his wife to ask her for a divorce, so that he could ask Catherine to marry him.

'If he had attempted to push me over the cliff I could not have been more startled,' wrote Catherine, to whom Keith's outburst was a re-run of Jim Dailey's deceit, and that of Dailey's replacement, her Harton-based dancing partner.

Keith was the third of her boyfriends to withhold the fact that he was promised to another. It was irrelevant that he was freeing himself to marry her. It was irrelevant in the boilerhouse of her emotions that she felt nothing much for him anyway. He had deceived her, and anyone less than true brought upon themselves all the ire born of Catherine's childhood trauma.

At the moment that unsuspecting Keith disgorged his good news, Catherine *became* Lena Mason – she remembered the hate she felt for Keith when she created her demented fictional character, a feeling which, in the novel, leads directly to the brutal murder of Alice Lovina, and in reality almost

'We'll go away from this cursed place,' Abel promises Alice, 'because for all its beauty the whole area has always been a cursed place to me. Will you? Will you Alice?'

The glorious cliff-top walk from Hastings through Fairlight Cove (she calls it a glen) to Winchelsea and Rye was chosen to establish the deception and violent emotions which motivate the novel because here Catherine's boyfriend, Keith, told her that he was married, and she very nearly pushed him over the cliff.

to Keith's demise, too: She went to hit out at him, to 'push him in the face. If I had done he would certainly have gone over the cliff, perhaps we both would have gone.'

Within weeks another man danced with her all evening at a workhouse 'do', and invited her to be his guest at a dinner party thrown by Mrs Silverlock.

Master Silverlock is seated fourth from the right in plus fours, next to Matron Silverlock. Catherine is on the far right.

Catherine had accepted the invitation and mentioned him to Matron, who had expressed surprise that he wasn't taking his wife. Catherine was dumfounded. But this was not the end of it. Another chap, again met at a workhouse party, a bit of a linguist – he had French, German, and was a student of Italian – came to meet her each day from work. And he, too, turned out to be married.

All this is omitted from the published version of *Our Kate*, and one has to wonder what we should make of these 'affairs' and two others with older men, of which she also makes mention. By her own account, sex was not an element in any of them. There is a suggestion that she was branded by one, in despair, as something of a tease. Above all she enjoyed sharpening her wit against men, and now she was beginning to be afraid of them – men were becoming people that you had to guard against.

If it *was* the protection and security of a father figure she was after, as I have suggested, then perhaps, too, there was a yen in Catherine to push all of them in the face for what her real father had denied her.

It is possible to detect through Catherine's writings a whole spectrum of feelings about the father she never knew. In her novel, *The Gillyvors* – Gillyvors, Catherine tells us are flowers known as nature's bastards – there is anger, fury even, that a father can consign his daughter to an eternity of ridicule and disdain as base-born. But as early as 1929, she seems to have come almost to a point of forgiveness, writing that her father could not have known at the time what suffering his selfish passion would cause her.

Years later, in *The Man Who Cried,* she discovered in the ecstasy and misery of Abel Mason's tears, the possibility of a mutual sense of loss: her father, who knew that Kate was with child, may have suffered, too. In so doing she came nearest to expressing her love for him.

But the novel wasn't written until the 1970s.

Forty years earlier, with Catherine buttoned against the cold of mankind, an Irish woman, 'with big heart and many endearing faults,' came into her life, and against this background of failed relationships Catherine found herself clinging to her, as she put it, 'like a drowning man to a raft.'

Annie Smyth first makes an appearance in the Governors Minutes at a meeting of the Sub Relief Committee, when a Contribution Order of six shillings weekly is made to her in the Municipal Hospital. A 'flu epidemic had taken hold of the workhouse. Shortly afterwards, the Assistant Matron handed in her notice and Catherine was asked to take over her duties. Now, with the duties of three officers on her hands, Catherine asked her staff to do overtime. None came forward, except Annie Smyth.

The irony was that Catherine had been trying to find a way of getting rid of Nan Smyth (as she was known). She had only been working in the laundry a short time, having been seconded from the hospital to cover for someone who was sick, but she was one of the most disruptive workers Catherine had. Nan's trick was to employ her native Irish humour, so that whenever she created a disturbance and Catherine sought to upbraid her, there'd be half the laundry behind her, enjoying a good laugh. Maybe it was Catherine's very Irishness that somehow gave Nan the confidence that she would, in the end, get the better of her. It was a Friday afternoon, machine cleaning duties were in progress, the Laundress had been called away, and when she returned, she found no work being done, only this Irish woman doing a sword dance over a pair of brooms.

Catherine was furious and decided to sack her formally on the following Monday, but was diverted and it was later that day that Matron gave Catherine licence to take on someone permanent to help her, and the Irish woman had applied. Catherine responded by telling her that she was lazy and had done more to impede work in the laundry than anyone, but Nan returned her look 'from deep attractive brown eyes, and in her masculine voice said, "You try me, Missis, and I'll show you."' And show her Nan did.

Nan had arrived at the workhouse in 1930, having run away from her Belfast home, her husband and her

Catherine at the time she made Nan Smyth her friend.

retarded daughter, Maisie. Now, under Catherine's personal direction, she appeared to turn over a new leaf, she had begun to work hard and show respect for her new boss, and before long she and Catherine actually became friends, not just work friends but tennis partners and companions. Eventually they became so inseparable that they decided to share a flat together. Catherine had been perplexed about Nan's child and, though Nan assured her that her sister was caring for her, it wouldn't be long before Maisie was sent for.

Clearly it was an odd friendship as perceived from within the workhouse – Nan literally a scrubber, Catherine head of the laundry – and Matron was aghast when Catherine told her they were moving in together.

Since John Smith, who was Catherine's first literary

Nan Smyth is seated far right, next to Kate and one away from Catherine. The photograph was taken in 1933.

agent at Christy & Moore, released a taped interview with his client about her relationship with Nan, there has been speculation that Nan and Catherine enjoyed a full, sexual relationship. In *The Girl From Leam Lane* I related Catherine's stories of how on two occasions women made direct lesbian advances to her, and she admitted to difficult relationships with her matrons, who seemed to cling to her. In *Our Kate* she lists a series of fears that characterised her emotional life, the last one of which, struck from the published edition, is the fear of women who tried to become closer to her than she would like. Women were drawn to her. She once said to me, 'I have had more trouble with women than with men, and goodness knows I've had enough trouble with them.'

Two factors which might be construed as evidence that Nan and Catherine enjoyed a sexual relationship are 1. that they slept in the same bed; and 2. that Nan had a masculine way about her. 'She was rather manly in her outlook and dress,' said Winnie Richardson, who met Nan in later years on a trip to see Catherine in Hastings, and hadn't liked her. 'She had hair parted in the middle and cut straight down,' said Cousin Teri, 'and mannish

tops.' Rosemary Barker told me that during the war Nan served in the army, for a time in South Shields, and cut the very figure of a Sergeant Major: 'She was very, very masculine. Her face was leathery and she always had a cigarette dangling from her mouth.'

Catherine declared openly that Nan loved her, and agreed that she was a masculine woman, but refuted the suggestion that she was a lesbian, adding that it was nothing special sleeping in the same bed, as she had always slept with her mother. Although Nan Smyth was the antithesis of anything relating to a mother, Catherine declared, twenty-five years later, that this was primarily the function Nan performed for her.

If true, dormitory arrangements – in what was, in any event, a one-room apartment – flowed from the fact that Catherine saw Nan as a mother substitute. It would be an extraordinary thing to say if not true.

Nan was older than Catherine and, in Cousin Sarah's words, 'the extreme opposite of what Kitty was trying to be at the time.' Like Kate, Nan was down to earth, 'jolly, exuberant...a bit feckless,' as John Smith said. But the 'mother' response flows, I think, from the undercurrents of their relationship. Both needed each other for their different reasons. From Nan, Catherine received the unconditional love characteristically associated with a mother for her child. Nan would do nothing to upset this fortuitous (or engineered) relationship. Her love for Catherine was unconditional because Nan couldn't afford to place any conditions on it. Catherine was her superior. Here was an opportunity to get out of the mess she was in. She was about to move into a flat with her boss, why wouldn't she be prepared to take anything Catherine threw at her at this time, and give back all that she had – her love – in return?

From Catherine's point of view, being loved by anyone was a whole new experience, and being loved unconditionally was probably the only way she could be loved. Certainly, later, her husband found that to be true.

In an unpublished manuscript of *Our Kate*, Catherine writes of Nan as a protector, a mother figure, but denies that she had a hold over her. She confessed herself incapable of earning another's love, and that is the point. Nan's love went *un*earned. This is why she was like a mother to her and why she was so important.

When Nan befriended her, it was, said Catherine, like an answer to a prayer, and events moved fast. Catherine was still living in the workhouse Lodge, but had retained her rented room in Clifton Road. One day, on a mission to pick up Catherine's tennis racket, Nan claimed to have discovered that her landlady had been double-renting Catherine's room. This occasioned Catherine's decision to move out of Clifton Road, and the subject came up of taking a flat with Nan.

The flat found was in West Hill, part of the Old Town – one large room and a kitchen with covered bath and lavatory. She and Nan moved into it in December 1931 and Catherine immediately set about decorating it, her interior design one that she claimed later was the best she had ever achieved. Her starting point had not seemed very promising, especially the black-painted woodwork and blue-papered walls, but with some heavy, dark pink curtains and a Chinese-style, grey carpet with black border, Catherine surpassed herself.

In the previous August, feeling much more settled, Catherine had returned home for the first time, for a week's holiday. She found the New Buildings unchanged except for a few new tenants and was surprised that she wanted it to remain like that, an unchanged, unchanging community. Not everyone had responded well to her – this may be a reference to the unpleasant business in Reny Harding's hairdressing salon, but her feelings were much more positive than when she had lived there, showing perhaps that her bid for freedom was serving to exorcise her demons. Kate was apparently not drinking, and the only other point she records is that her mother showed an interest in visiting Hastings.

Kate arrived in Hastings the following year, 1932. She arrived sober and claimed not to have touched a drop since McMullen's burial, which pleased Catherine. She was taken to the workhouse and impressed everyone except Matron, who had become a receptor for Catherine's feelings about her mother and may simply have said what she thought Catherine wanted to hear. All went surprisingly well, and naturally Kate got on with Nan like a house on fire.

Kate and Nan were out of the same pod, and later in her stay Nan suggested that Kate leave the North and move to Hastings too – not a suggestion that was likely if she was enjoying a rampant physical relationship with her daughter, incidentally, but, given her immediate empathy with Kate, one that would, if implemented, redress the balance of power at home, reducing Nan's need to kowtow to Catherine, for Kate was always more likely to take Nan's part.

From Catherine's point of view it was a disastrous scenario. Her independence from Kate, and all that that entailed, would be lost. But there she was, proudly showing her how she had got everything together so successfully. Could she now say that it would not withstand the presence of her own mother on the scene? Was not Kate a reformed character? In any case, how could she refuse Kate while she was standing there, stone cold sober, laughing and enjoying life with her and Nan? Both Kate and Nan had played it well.

The upshot was a move to a bigger flat in the same block and Kate's arrival to live with them on a permanent basis. When Catherine greeted her mother off the train, she saw at once the depth of error she had made, for Kate was reeling drunk.

Kate's coming may have been a disaster for Catherine, but to her credit she tried to turn the problem to advantage. She knew she had to get Kate away from

In the move from Hastings Old Town to the Hurst, Catherine was moving from the seaside to the country in those days. Even today, left, there are rural surprises behind the greatly increased number of houses in the area.

Hastings Old Town, an area notorious for the number of pubs relative to its population. Indeed, at this precise moment in time there was a public campaign to cut the number. So it was that she put the lease on the flat up for sale and set in motion a plan to buy a house in a more remote, residential quarter, which the three of them might run as a business.

7 BREAKDOWN

*The Hurst in 1911. The Estate Agent's claims for the house as a
'gentleman's residence' rested on its ownership by a certain
Colonel Alexander Burton-Brown FRAS, FCS.*

That the purchase of property was even on the cards seems extraordinary, but
Catherine had always been good with money. She hated the waste of it, perhaps
because there was little around and Kate wasted so much of it on drink and she knew
personally just how hard it was to earn it. From an early age she had kept a watchful
eye over it, walking instead of taking a tram and saving her pennies, attaching a frugal
strategy to the dreams she had for a better life. There was a canny respect for its
investment potential, too. At eight she bought, for the price of a few pence, a policy
from the shipping offices at Tyne Dock to insure her own life for £50. It was all part
of the self-disciplined mind set, destined to make good, which in later life always
tackled the fundamental material things first, head on, before moving on to the more
interesting things.

Maybe, while she was still living on Tyneside, she had benefited from advice
from Jim Dailey, who had been a broker. Whatever, by 1932, she had a policy with
Sun Life of Canada worth £1,000, and she mortgaged this to secure her dream house,
The Hurst in Hoads Wood Road. She bought it even before she had sold the lease on
her flat, and into it moved her mother and Nan, and Nan's daughter, Maisie, who had
been shipped over from Ireland.

'Gentleman's residence' were the words the Estate agent had used. He had
been trying to flog it for five years. It was a disaster of a property, woodworm, rot,
leaking roofs – in hopeless disrepair, but it was big with turrets and multiple roofs

and rooms – fifteen of them, including a spacious drawing room with floor to ceiling sash windows, a butler's pantry, even a wine cellar, and – joy of joys – a huge garden leading down the hill.

In practical terms it left a lot to be desired, however: 'The Hurst was a big gaping house, with wooden floors and big kitchens, a cold place. I can remember going into a backyard to get into the kitchen,' recalls Cousin Sarah. 'It was flamin' cold, I know that much. Cor, dear oh dear,' said Cousin Teri.

Today when you go up to the top floor and look out of The Hurst, all you can see leading down the hill are roofs of smaller houses, though in 1933 The Hurst had been one of only a few houses on Hoads Wood Road.

Altogether, The Hurst today is a sad relic of what it was in 1911, when owned by Colonel Alexander Burton-Brown FRAS, FCS. He lived there with his wife, Ethel Augusta, their daughter, Jean, and stepson, Rupert Noel-Clarke.

Looking out from the top floor of The Hurst today, over what was once the full extent of its garden, domesticity ranges down the hill as far as the eye can see in what was, in 1933, open countryside.

Five years later, when Catherine's relationship with Nan had foundered, she sold off part of the garden for building and used the money to buy alternative accommodation for Nan and to pay off Kate's numerous debts.

Sixty years later it was converted into a Residential Home, those massive rooms have been split into dozens of smaller ones, an unsightly extension has been built on to the front and those grand, floor to ceiling sash windows have been ripped out and replaced with plastic monstrosities. Oddly, the present occupiers have never been able to find the wine cellar.

The tumultuous interpersonal goings-on that followed Kate's arrival on the scene in 1932 up to the point when Nan was parcelled off in 1938, would fill more than one novel. Basically, Catherine became Kate and Nan's meal ticket, and Nan milked her for all she could get. Catherine would work a full shift at the workhouse and then came home to knock the place into shape, the idea being to take in residents, for The Hurst became a cross between an old people's home, a nursing home and a guest house, with these three women, all quite extraordinary in their own way, running it with various staff, including a cook called Mrs Webster.

Of course it was in this house that Catherine courted her future husband, Tom Cookson, and he lived there from 1937 as a paying guest. 'They had blind people staying and mentally handicapped people,' remembers Cousin Sarah, as well as other guests. There were seven for certain in 1938, including a TB

Catherine demonstrating her fencing prowess to some of the residents of The Hurst. Since she began to work on herself in Harton Institution, Catherine had become an accomplished human being, physically and intellectually – 'She was everything really,' recalls Tony Weeks-Pearson, 'a fencer, a painter, a writer...'

patient, a man in his late thirties who was soon to die. He is memorable because of the impact he had on Catherine's confidence as a writer. He was reckoned to be something of an intellectual and he and Catherine would have long discussions about books and ideas, so it was perfectly natural for Catherine to ask him, one day, whether he would read one of her stories. She had not stopped writing since leaving the North, and there were stacks of short stories and sketches of life in the workhouse, written (so Tom told me many years later) in the style of the *Hamilton* series, which she kept in a cupboard on the landing. The fellow read one of these and whatever he actually said,

Catherine's first notion was to turn The Hurst into a home for epileptics, running this in tandem with her responsibilities at the workhouse, where she supervised eleven permanent staff and up to thirty inmates as well as taking her share of responsibility for the daily casuals and tramps from the road. As it developed, however, she took blind people, a TB patient and a variety of guests with nothing obviously wrong with them at all.

Catherine was so upset that she burned all her work on a fire.

Tom's sister, Edna Humphreys, can remember visiting the house in the late 1930s: 'We spent a week in Hastings just before the Second War was declared, there was Joan [sister] and myself and a neighbour went down and when Elizabeth [daughter] was a baby we spent a week at The Hurst then. I remember the place at the top of the house [under the turreted roof] which was demolished after the war because it was damaged. I remember the gorgeous grounds, the big kitchen, oh I can picture it! When we went there, there was Pansy and about three people Catherine was looking after. Pansy didn't seem quite 10 pence to a shilling. There was also the housekeeper, she was deaf. I never met Nan Smyth. I don't think she was on the scene at the time.'

Indeed, she was not. Houses next to The Hurst today are built on what was then Catherine's garden. In 1938 she had had to sell the land in order to get shot of Nan.

At the start, the main problem had not been Nan, but Kate. With no pubs in the area, she would bring drink home, and get out of hand with the guests. Tanked up to the eyeballs she indulged in her particular talent as a practical joker. She might smear jam on door handles or bake a pie crust with surprise ingredients instead of meat. 'I think Kitty used to get mad at her,' said Cousin

Kate in 1935 at the height of her drunken antics and practical jokes, and shortly before her banishment to the West Hill flat.

Teri with understatement. 'But Kate would make people laugh. She was a great cook. And she was a great person as a boarding house keeper. She just had her little lapses sometimes…' Kate would also invite her own friends down from Shields, and then slink off to her favourite Hastings pub, the Hole In The Wall, leaving Mrs Flannagan or Aunt Mary or Teri to look after the guests.

It must have seemed to Catherine that half of East Jarrow had re-entered her life. David McDermott would of course also be down when on leave, and it was one of his hobnail boots that Kate threw at Catherine – it missed her head by inches – after a particularly heavy drinking session. The problem was that mother and daughter did not get on, they seemed to operate from entirely different bases. Kate was for living life moment-to-moment, day-to-day; she had no reason to think that life could be lived in any other way. But Catherine had plans. Besides the workhouse and The Hurst and the guests, she also still found time to write, and continued to educate and improve herself. Kate's way may have seemed like fun to others, but it was simply not hers.

In 1935, the relationship reached total breakdown. Catherine became suicidal and Kate agreed that she should move out. Fortunately, the lease on the flat in West Hill had still not been sold, so Catherine signed it over to her mother and Kate moved in there and took in paying guests. For a time they kept out of the way of each other and Catherine was surprised to hear that Kate had swapped the lease on the flat for one on a large terraced house. It was there, on her way to her weekly, hour-long fencing lesson, that Catherine first met Tom, who had come to Hastings in the autumn of 1936 to take up the job of Maths master at the local Grammar School. Kate, who had already been at the whisky before Catherine arrived, had told her she wanted to show her off to him. Catherine had better things to do than be looked over by one of Kate's guests and was on her way out when her mother threw open the door of the sitting room and bellowed at Tom that her daughter was here to meet her.

Tom rose and said, 'How do you do?'

Doris Johnson makes the interesting point that Catherine's very odd response to this was spontaneous, and may be more revealing than one might suppose. Her reported words were: 'Do you fence?'

Catherine, Tom and Kate during this period. Although her mother introduced Catherine's future husband to her, when she saw that the relationship was becoming serious and that soon she and Nan would lose their meal ticket, they devised a devilish strategy to turn Catherine against him. For a short time it succeeded.

What made her say that? Suppose Tom had been able to fence, would she have invited him to join the class? Or was she, as Doris suggests, not talking about fencing at all. Was she, a person who adored fencing, provocatively asking the man to whom she was instantly attracted, 'Will you share my pleasures?'

And did Tom kick himself especially hard when he failed to rise to the opportunity offered him? His response was simply, 'No,' and Catherine turned on her heel and walked out.

Certainly the episode pricked Tom Cookson into action. He was a shy man by nature, not timid, but shy, and yet within two days of meeting her he realised he couldn't get her out of his head and made what was for him the boldest of plays. Years later he told Tyne Tees Television that the day after his first meeting with Catherine he was restless and realised he had to hear and see her again. That was the order in which she had appealed to his senses. There was something about her accent that had beguiled him, what he called the 'lilt of the Northeast'. Only later did he see that she was a beautiful woman too.

Two nights after first meeting her this shy unassuming man found himself standing at the front door of The Hurst clutching an evening paper and asking Catherine to the cinema. Altogether, it seems to me, a situation of pure romance, but for shy Tom it was brazen in the extreme. The denouement fits Doris's analysis perfectly. For Catherine was pleased to have the evening paper and accepted Tom's invitation to the cinema. Despite all her waffle to us in *Our Kate* about how busy she was and how absurd was the idea of the match, she accepted Tom's invitation immediately, without further ado. They went to the cinema and afterwards they walked the two miles home and sat either side of the fire, talking until the hall clock struck twelve, when, in Cinderella fashion, they kissed and knew in that moment that it was right.

So, who was this Tom Cookson? I turned to his half-sister, Edna, to find out. Tom was the son of Thomas Cookson, a verger at a church in Chingford, Essex, who had died in 1915. 'Tom was 2, 3 [born in 1912] when his father died, he must have been born in Chingford. There was Jack, the eldest boy, Tom and sister Mabel. My parents married in 1920, Tom's father died in Grays so my mother was already living there and they were married there. Grays is on the north bank of the Thames [close to Tilbury Docks]. The second father, my dad, died the same year as Kennedy, 1963. He was killed on the Friday. Dad died on the Saturday morning.'

Tom had adored his second father, a plumber's mate, and learned from him practical skills put to good use when he and Catherine were tackling The Hurst. He had been schooled at Palmers in Gray's, the local Grammar School. 'He always had a wicked sense of humour,' said Edna, which is not something I had noticed in him in later years. 'I must have been 8 or 9 when he went up to Oxford. There were only two of us [Edna and Mabel] when he went and then Jean was born in 1934. I remember them saying nothing about Jean's birth until Tom came home and found her there. Mother had to go to work to keep him at Oxford and so when he came home he virtually looked after us girls. I can

The front door of The Hurst. 'The next day, on a trumped-up excuse, I called at her home. Would she like to go to the pictures? Yes, she would.' recalled Tom.

remember him shutting me in the cupboard. I must have got a bit cheeky to him, and I remember one day doing it again and shutting myself in the cupboard before he could. There was no smacking, no abuse at all, but I knew the punishment. He was very firm, and I remember he came up to a funeral – was it Dad or Mum? – and Elizabeth, my daughter, was getting ready for her "O levels" and she was a bit flummoxed with Maths and he took her off and when she came back she said, "Oh it's so easy. I know what to do now, and she just sailed through then."'

There are some quirky coincidences of names in Tom and Catherine's life, which seem to bind the two together even before they met. Palmers, of course, was also the name of the shipyard at Jarrow, which Catherine knew so well. She had grown up within a stone's throw of Cookson's Glassworks on the Tyne, and as Kate drew to Catherine's attention in the 1950s, there had also been a Cookson lead works. 'Yes do you Remember, those Rail Crossings top of Western Road on the way to Hebburn it was up there.' Now, Tom's college at Oxford turned out to be St Catherine's.

This confused me when I first learned of it because I knew that St Catherine's was only founded in the 1960s. In fact, in Tom's day, it did not have full college status within the university. It was a non-collegiate Society, which offered opportunities to win Oxford University degrees to underprivileged students without the means to pay full college fees. As a Society it had no buildings of its own and none of the trademark Oxbridge college traditions. Tom, I discovered, gained a First Class degree in Mods and two years later, in 1935, just as Kate was being dismissed from The Hurst for her drunken antics, graduated with a good Second Class Honours degree in Mathematics.

So, like Catherine, Tom had come from a poor background, and in the crucial years (3 to 8) he had grown up without a father. The elements in Tom, noted by everyone, were a gentle firmness and a selfless, supportive nature. Perhaps these characteristics were fostered in his role as surrogate father to his siblings, certainly they were proven in his role as schoolmaster. When I told an ex-pupil of his, Tony Weeks-Pearson, that I was writing a book about Catherine, he put it this way: 'Books should really be about the Tom Cooksons of this world. Because, you know, Tom is at the heart of this in relation to Kitty, not just as a husband but as a complete factotum, whether it was cooking or as amanuensis or whatever. Everything that Tom did, he did for her... It wasn't just giving up his time for me and dozens of other boys, listening or advising or spending time with them, it was just the same with *anyone* he met, and it was the same with Kitty Cookson. I always thought theirs was a more professional relationship of husband and wife – his aiding her – even more so than it was with us. You see, you used to forget that he was a teacher, he took a *personal* interest...very supportive.'

Catherine at 30, the year she first met Tom Cookson. When he arrived in Hastings to take up the position of Master of Mathematics at the Grammar School, Catherine was away in France visiting a French woman, who had been a guest at the Hurst and had introduced her to Voltaire.

Catherine was serious about educating herself and had been starved of intellectual stimulus at the Hurst before Tom arrived.

Doris also made the point: 'Tom gave her all the things she needed – nurturing, parenting. She would be able to show her vulnerable side to him.' Parenting was what Catherine had been seeking in her relationships all along.

When I pursued Tom's highly individual interpretation of his role as teacher in and out of the classroom with some other of his pupils, they offered the following reports:

'He was my teacher in the A stream. He was very small, a very tiny guy, but he had a presence about him that was quite compelling. There was something very gentle…and yet he had the ability to command the attention and respect of a group of thirty adolescents.' (Steve Blower)

'Mr. Cookson was my Maths master. I remember him as a teacher who had a knack of explaining in a very understandable manner… He was very quiet in manner, but was well able to control us if we tried to get a bit unruly.' (John Finch)

'I remember him stressing that we should not worry about being confined in the C stream because we might well end up in the best seat. "Boys in the A stream," he said, "would go on to serious occupations, earn little money and probably ride bicycles to work. Boys in the B stream would be teachers or civil servants and drive secondhand cars. But you in the C stream are going to be the businessmen and drive brand new cars." He was absolutely right. I went into the army, then set up in the pub trade, sold up and retired by the age of 52!' (James Davidson)

But what about initial impressions? How slayed had Catherine been by Tom's physical proportions? In *Maggie Rowan* she pours scorn on small men. In Maggie's dreams her men are 'tall and strong and virile', having a short husband is something at which people laugh. This is the macho myth of the Northern man. Just how important it was to Catherine is not clear, but Tom stood five foot four and a half inches and one has to recall her comment about 'squirts of pitmen' in respect of Lily Maguire's father.

On the face of it, Tom hardly matched up to the Robinsons, the renowned South Shields family of boxers, with all the chutzpa and fierce loyalty of a Mafiosi family from Brooklyn, into which Francie Nichol married at around this time, and whom she describes in her autobiography, *Francie*. Catherine might have caught a whiff of this scene because there was boxing in the tram sheds on the edge of the New Buildings. Francie's Johnny became featherweight champion of the North of England, but died tragically at 24. His father, Henry, was heavyweight champion of the North, his uncle lightweight champ of all England, and his grandfather, Peter, 'the biggest and the hardest of the lot of them'. He had made his money in fairground boxing booths before bringing the family to South Shields.

The Robinsons' cavernous house in Shields was furnished with specially large pieces of furniture to accommodate the scale of humanity that passed through it. They epitomised the real macho Tyneside culture, of which brawlers like the McMullens were a poor imitation.

But, actually, that was the paradox in Tom, because he was himself a

In the 1930s, besides boxing and football, in which he had a Blue from Oxford, Tom Cookson became involved in school cricket, where the team was so good it had to be banned from competing for the Argus Cup.

'I remember him as a teacher who had a knack of explaining the subject in a very understandable manner – not easy to do in Maths! He was very quiet in manner, but was well able to control us if we tried to get a bit unruly.' John Finch, ex-pupil

'You used to forget that he was a teacher... he took a personal interest in me, that was at the heart of my going to Oxford and got me into teaching eventually. He was a very good footballer. When I first saw him play it was quite clear from the first few moves he made that he was ace, he was a small, fast, dribbling man on the field.' Tony Weeks-Pearson, ex-pupil

'He was very small, a very tiny guy, but he had a presence about him that was quite compelling.' Steve Blower, ex-pupil

'I shall always remember, he said: "Boys in the A stream will go on to serious occupations, earn little money and probably ride bicycles to work. Boys in the B stream will be teachers or civil servants and drive secondhand cars. But you in the C stream are going to be the businessmen and drive brand new cars." He was absolutely right.' James Davidson, ex-pupil

boxer, and he started up a Boxing Club in Hastings Grammar School, which at one time boasted as many as eighty members.

'He was quite a sportsman,' remembers Edna of her brother as a boy, 'though he was small. I still remember his two friends coming to collect him for school and they towered above him and they'd always walk either side of him. It was so funny. But he played football and tennis and water polo at Oxford. Then I've got a photograph of him playing in the Varsity match, football. And I have got his Blue, which he got in football. And of course he played cricket as well.'

'He was a very good footballer,' agreed ex-pupil Tony. 'When I first saw him play it was quite clear from the first few moves he made that he was ace, he was a small, fast, dribbling man on the field.'

Tom arrived in September 1936 as replacement for Michael Jerrom, whose extra-curricular responsibilities included Football, Scouts and the Drama Society. From the start he was closely associated with sport, which meant that he refereed the 'Scratch-Sixes', a gruelling tradition since 1891 of half hourly or 20-minute six-a-side games of football. As Manager of the football team he is recalled by Baines and Conisbee in the school's *History*, as displaying a special touch: 'Behind T H Cookson's cheery countenance lurked a hundred schemes for gingering up the team and outwitting the enemy.' Besides his boxing enterprise and football, he was also involved in cricket, in which the school already had so powerful a team that in the summer of 1936 they had to be removed from the Argus Cup competition, 'as members belonged to much too high a class.'

Tom arrived at the school in September 1936 as replacement for Michael Jerrom, the master responsible for Football, Scouts and the Drama Society. From the start he was closely associated with sport, and introduced boxing to the school.

Catherine galvanised people's lives. In the years leading up to the Second War, The Hurst became a centre for dramatic interludes and parties.

When Tom came into Catherine's life, she had been some four years with Nan and had given up the idea of ever getting married. She was a single, self-sufficient woman, who had a large house and business to run, as well as a well-paid, responsible job. But all that was swept aside when they met, Catherine claiming that they knew at once that 'we were for each other.'

This didn't come as good news to Nan, who had already had her nose put out of joint by the banishment of Kate. In the early stages of the relationship with Tom, Nan appears to have done all she could to belittle him, no doubt

Kate can be seen close to the centre of the line-up, where she could generally be found when there was a party going on at The Hurst.

beginning with his small physical stature, which may well be the source of the *Maggie Rowan* quote. On one occasion, Catherine had been going with Tom to a dance, and Nan threatened to hang herself if she did, causing such a scene that Catherine sat up fighting with her until two o'clock in the morning.

She responded to Tom's appearance like a 'woman scorned', teaming up with Kate in a determined strategy to keep Catherine from marrying him, even tampering with his mail to find information she could use to reduce his credibility in Catherine's eyes.

She even succeeded for a while, forcing him out of The Hurst. When Tom returned and he and Catherine re-united, she started her hate campaign all over again.

Then, in 1938, Catherine made a decisive move, she sold part of the garden to raise some cash, paid off Kate's debts, which had reached worrying proportions, dispatched her back to South Shields, and set Nan up in a house of her own.

It was the end of her mother, as far as Catherine was concerned and she would have nothing more to do with her until well after the war. Alas, it was the end of David McDermott, too. In the same year he fell off the quayside on the way back to his ship and was drowned.

Nan fared well, turning Catherine's gift of a house into a capital earner, buying and selling property, and finally ending up in a 'beautiful big stone house called Elphinstone Court with a great big drive,' as Cousin Sarah recalled from their first meeting in 1946. 'She was married to an Irish fellow and she had a daughter who was a backward girl. She would have these old green dungarees on, untidy, but she made a lot of money, entertained the racing set a lot. Maybe being Irish she had some sort of connection with the racing fraternity. There was a lot of division even as late as when I used to go down. Kitty never said, but there must have been an up-and-downer. Kate and her hadn't wanted Kitty to marry Tom, because Kitty was the breadwinner...'

In this post-war period, Nan appeared to have access to a great deal of money, which Sarah always assumed she had made on the horses. Certainly Nan became a great entertainer of the horse racing set before the whole thing collapsed and she was bankrupted.

'The last time I saw Nan Smyth she was in a dirty little place on the front. Kitty said she had lived it up

'*She was very, very masculine. Her face was leathery and she always had a cigarette dangling from her mouth.*'
    '*The last time I saw Nan Smyth she was in a dirty little place on the sea front. When all the money was gone she had no friends and she had to sell everything.*'

with her racing friends [gambling] and when all the money was gone she had no friends and she had to sell everything.'

The temptation is to see more than a bit of Dorrie Clarke, the twisted, resentful busybody in *Kate Hannigan,* in the pre-war Nan Smyth. She it is who steals six letters from Kate Hannigan and gives them to Stella Prince in order to prevent Kate marrying Rodney, the love of her life. Nan and letters and bitter resentment certainly go hand in hand. On her death bed she would direct Tom to a bunch of them in a drawer in that down-at-heel, basement flat on Hastings sea front, letters which, as we shall see, had been saved with one purpose in mind, to break up Tom and Catherine's relationship from beyond the grave, even a quarter century or more after they were married.

It was from this that Tom had rescued Catherine. In July 1939 Catherine left her job at the workhouse and

The Roman Catholic Church of St Mary, Star of the Sea in Hastings, where Catherine and Tom were married on June 1, 1940, shortly before Catherine's thirty-fourth birthday. Tom was six years younger.

later that year she offered The Hurst as home to a crowd of blind evacuees. Then, when news came through that the Grammar School was to up sticks and move to St Albans in Hertfordshire for the duration of the war, Catherine at last made up her mind to marry Tom, and on June 1, 1940, they made their vows.

Through marriage to Tom, Catherine gained a new kind of respect, for what is lost to time is that Tom was the one well known in Hastings then,

'Everyone respected him in the town,' said Josephine Austin, who knew them. 'That was something Catherine gained, tremendous respect because she married Tom.' But Catherine would never shine in the light of another party.

There could not have been a worse start to Tom and Catherine's marriage. The facts are well known. In July, 1940, they took a flat in Victoria Street, St Albans. On December 7, their first baby was born three months prematurely, dead.

This had a terrible psychological effect on Catherine. She refers to the child, whom they named David, in a diary she began to keep in February, 1942:

David didn't get a chance to live. I wonder if God looks after babies of six months, I absolutely refuse to believe they go to Limbo. Its just about a year since Tom took me to see his grave, I remember how sick I felt when the man told us he was in a general grave, together with three men and an old woman, who I gathered had come from the Union. He wasn't allowed a grave because he hadn't been baptised... he had looked so sweet the first and only time I saw him, but then I thought – the old woman will look after him, and she will be so pleased to find a baby with her – fanciful, but it helped to ease the hurt.

Catherine and Tom lost four babies between 1940 and 1945, and this tragic intertwining of love and death cheated Catherine of becoming a mother just as she had been cheated of *having* a mother by the dissemblance at her birth. Once again, a family had been denied her.

In the period leading up to their marriage, Catherine had begun questioning her faith in a series of meetings with the local Roman Catholic priest, who had shaken her by advising that she and Tom should not be married in a Catholic church unless Tom converted to Roman Catholicism.

In following her descent into nervous breakdown, it is vital to appreciate how vulnerable this questioning of her faith made Catherine in the lead-up to losing her first baby. Her faith had been the only positive constant to balance the negative, self-destructive tendencies of her damaged disposition. Religion may have one of the least happy profiles in human history, but faith has also promoted unity within sections of mankind and within individual psyches. When not co-opted for purposes of power, religion is a unifying force, and it had certainly proved to be so during the trauma of Catherine's early years. Indeed, as I have shown, it introduced her to the notion of selfless love, which might otherwise have remained a stranger to her personality.

Now, as in history, so in Catherine's life, faith was being muddied in the turbulent waters of sectarianism. The narrow-minded priest was telling her she couldn't marry the man she loved unless Tom lied about his beliefs. So, she was discarding it. Fortunately, Tom was on hand to fill the vacuum with his love. He had, indeed, encouraged Catherine's questioning of Catholicism, seeing it as feeding her disquiet. But then came the loss of their child and she began to see David's death as punishment for her lack of faith. Worse still, the war was about to split the lovers up. Catherine would soon be all alone again.

In August 1941, Tom enlisted in the RAF and was stationed first in Leicester for training, and then in Sleaford, Lincolnshire, where Catherine became pregnant again and suffered a miscarriage, having barely recovered from the first tragedy less than a year earlier. Tom was then posted to RAF Madley near Hereford. Catherine took digs at No. 1 Ryelands Street in the city and here, alone, her fears redoubled on her.

The doors of St Peter & Paul's, Tyne Dock. Catherine had shut out religion, but the grief they both felt over the loss of another baby combined with Tom's increasing concern over Catherine's state of mind to lead to an about turn.

February, 1942
– It is 6.30 and I am sitting by the fire – everything looks so bright and clean – the furniture is shining – the brasses are gleaming – it is so comfortable yet there is no-one to notice – but me. He is in a cold wooden hut, and he is not well [he has a cold]. We didn't ask much out of life only to be together – but the world is at war so he has to live in a wooden hut and I in this little flat.'

Their enforced separation, the grief they both felt over the loss of another baby, the inner tussle over her faith, the uncertainty of war combined with Tom's increasing concern over his wife's stability to lead to a decision to do an about turn and promote religion as her help. He wrote:

I really wanted to go to Mass yesterday morning, for I have prayed so hard lately, and I think I have prayed fervently. I'll go on praying for you my Darling one, praying that nothing physical nor mental harm, or agony should come to you, praying that you might always be happy, that you get all you deserve. I always tell Our Lady that you are so good, and that you deserve so much. I should not use the word deserve for she knows best how she'll intercede for you. But she knows what I mean To a certain extent it makes me feel easier in my mind to think that I can talk to her, and through her to you. You know that I would never have said I felt like this, unless I really did. Perhaps it seems too big a transformation to you – But certain things can happen in a flash – actually in my case it has been a comparatively gradual transformation, and it has all been through you. It did seem funny to me to think how much prayer meant to you but now I know Sweetheart, and I have to thank you for showing me – [The transformation] is born with the realisation of how you loved me, that I should be given this great love for you, and to know that it was reciprocated just had to have something behind it – for my sweetheart you are divine, as divine as you'll ever be even after death. I just think of you as being so big – so big in heart and mind, so big in giving, so big in everything that matters in life for me –

After quoting from his letter in her diary, Catherine recalled that Tom hadn't believed in God back in 1937 when they first met. She then asked God for forgiveness for 'the thoughts that I still harbour, namely that there are a lot of flaws in it [Christianity] – but still that isn't God's fault, it is man's and are they flaws?'

She then described the beautiful Church of the Holy Cross at Leicester, which she had attended with Tom, praising the 'flow of fine modulated language from the pulpit – a cross between a reformed B Shaw and H G Wells,' before complaining about the seating – all the seats facing the altar were reserved and 'paid' for – 'I wanted to crack their necks for them, many a Sunday morning during my four months stay in Leicester…'

Her diary speaks poignantly of the pain of a woman denied the experience of a loving family as a child and now being denied the chance of creating one with the man she loved. For all her doubts, her lament is inextricably bound up with religion at the symbolic level: 'When I was mentally desperate, I begged the mother figure to come to my aid. I lit countless candles; I had masses said. All to no avail.'

It is February 15, Catherine is waiting in Ryelands street for Tom, due home for a weekend's leave from RAF Madley. Their plan is to create a child, a human form that would take the place of David in her heart:

While I was waiting for Tom coming I knelt by the bedroom fire – and my mind kept straying off the [rosary] beads – thinking if I am to have a child dear Lord, grant that will be healthy and good, grant that there will never be any wars for him to fight in, give him his father's brains and his kind and sweet disposition, give him a strong sense of justice and of tolerance, and dear Lord I said apologetically with a smile, give him my sense of humour –

At 9.00 he came in, so tired, so dirty and so hungry. While he held me tight and long in his arms, I could only think 'My Dear, my Dear'. He would hold me at arms length then pull me close to him, until I protested. What a supper I had for him, soup, rump steak (my whole week's rations), bacon and sausages, fried bread and then a trifle, but he didn't eat as much as I wanted him to, I think he was so excited at seeing me, yet it wasn't three weeks since he went away, but it has seemed such a long time. After supper we sat by the fire in the kitchen and talked of many things – I didn't say to him what I was thinking – what I thought so often, that I always had that weird feeling that I would never see the end of the war. This wasn't just a feeling of depression since Tom had joined up in August. I had had it since the very beginning of the war – and even before when the dread of war was afloat – but of course I didn't say anything, I just let him talk about 'The Hurst' and what we would do when we went back He became quite serious about having the lawn made into flower beds – and all the time – [I was thinking] 'what does it matter'.

And then we went to bed. The pleasure I got from seeing him stretch his 5, 5 1/2 and exclaim, 'Oh Darling, sheets!' He lay in my arms quietly, like a child making little grunting noises, which he always does when he is happy. He talked at intervals, saying silly things such as I was the most beautiful woman in the world, that out of all God's creatures there wasn't one to compare with me, that never in his wildest dreams had he thought to get anyone like me for a wife, a dream woman come to life – he said it haltingly – for words don't come to him easily, and of course it wasn't true but I was touched and pleased. Then I made him happy, and I lay in his arms and he stroked my hair to send me off to sleep as he always does, and I forgot everything but the warmth of his body – and it was morning.

In the next entry she wonders whether they have made a baby. Tom has gone. She receives the news of the fall of Singapore and sinks into a deep depression for the mothers of the sons who are lost. Then she begins to talk to her child, her would-be Valentine baby, naming him then and there, Valentino: 'I don't think I am particularly fond of the name, Valentino,' she writes. 'I would rather have David, but then David died, David didn't get a chance to live...' The following day she receives a letter from Tom: 'What a grand weekend I've had dearest one. Really Darling it was just too wonderful for words. To see that look in your eyes when I opened the door was like an invitation to paradise – and so it was. All the heaviness that had been growing in me fell away completely, and I was again in my beloved's arms – I was again kissing her beautiful face, and her voice was playing the most wonderful music in my ears – I have a little body, but my heart just seems to swell right out of it when I am with you.' Catherine put her hand on her tummy and murmured, 'Do you know Valentino it isn't two years till June since your father and I were married – yet it seems a happy lifetime – I can't work back to a time when we weren't together, so completely has he wiped out all the past from my mind.'

There was no Valentino. They lost their third child in 1943, and Catherine was alone once more. She fell into a desperate paroxysm of loneliness and was bleeding heavily from the nose almost daily. Still the cause had not been diagnosed. Again, she turned to her God for help: 'I lit candles to Our Lady, who I understood was the mother of God (yet who had not been recognised for centuries after her son's death). I bought a number of Masses, oh yes, you had to pay for having a Mass said. But I recall there was a very civilised priest in Hereford at that time, and he talked to me so quietly and nicely. And strangely we became friends. But it was no good. There was a battle raging in me, not only about religion but about myself. My illegitimacy was hitting me harder then than at any other time. It was because, I think, I was physically so low. I had been losing blood practically every day since I was 18. My nose-bleeding caused anaemia. I must have been in a very low state at that time. My health suffered the loss of three babies in the three years that we had been married.'

She became 'as thin as two lathes'. On top of everything there will have been misplaced guilt at depriving Tom of fatherhood. He had given her so much and she was not capable of such a fundamental thing as giving him the child he so wanted. Nevertheless, she took hold of herself and found a job in a munitions factory, before having to leave when she developed an allergy to cordite, the explosives material with which she was working. 'Then, still education bent, I actually became a commercial artist for J Arthur Dixon [who was based] in the Isle of Wight. I had discovered I had a talent. I could turn pencils, academy chalk and carbon crayon into an impression of an etching. Moreover I had taken to the piano again and was working towards an exam.'

The commission from J Arthur Dixon was to illustrate Arthur Mee's *Kings' England* and came after a local printer had seen Catherine's drawings of St Albans Abbey and Hereford Cathedral and suggested she turn her hand to postcards. She was also working towards an art exam, taking lessons from a painter called André van der Meersch. But what had at first seemed like an encouraging way in which she could bury her grief in a project, became tiring and more unrewarding even than the pen painting in William Black Street. The

This picture of Catherine during the period of her separation from Tom, leading up to her breakdown in 1945, is in stark contrast to the one on page 123, taken just a few years later when she had begun to find success as a writer, though right up until the time I met her in August 1985 the battle continued within: 'I put on this front, this act that everything was quite normal… But underneath I was writhing in fear. The shadows never leave you, you know.'

cards made her a halfpenny each and the Arthur Mee illustrations were to be so small that she had to draw them under a magnifying glass.

She was running in ever decreasing circles and the climax came when she fell and hurt her leg. The fall caused phlebitis – inflammation of veins in the leg. After being diagnosed, Catherine was told to go to bed. Then, after three days, she was told by another doctor to get up…then to go to bed again. She lay for weeks in her lonely room. Her landlady was not of a very sympathetic nature, for most of the time there was no-one in the house except for her landlady's father, a very old man. Tom in the Air Force was at RAF Madley or, indeed, teaching. For the best part of the next six weeks she lay rigidly still so as not to disturb the damaged leg. A nurse came in to wash her, otherwise she passed the time practising for her art exam, and thinking thoughts that were doing her no good at all.

She began to see her life as a hopeless stream of attempts to anaesthetise herself against the hurt she felt inside, which she associated with the stigma of illegitimacy, and which, up to now, had always driven her on. All the effort of her bid for freedom, her leaving Tyneside, her reading, her writing, her art, all the hours pushing herself at the workhouse to make good, the effort of getting The Hurst up and running, where had any of it got her? Fragile respectability, a veneer, a momentary sense of achievement which left untouched the vacuum inside, the aloneness to which she had been consigned by lovelessness and the 'loss' of her mother at birth.

Now, of course, nothing would have been less likely to console her than the possibility of a reunion with Kate. As far as she was concerned, she had done with her mother for good. There would be no late re-connection of the primal unity. It had been rent asunder in trauma, and the attempt to heal the scars had failed in Hastings. The hate and resentment left by the 'fracture' of her birth was more deeply rooted now than they had ever been, for every approach to unity within had failed. Her writing and her art had got her nowhere. Her love for Tom had been cauterised by the loss of three babies. It was not enough for her to suffer the lovelessness of her own birth, she had to have a body impervious to the love of its own offspring.

Even the Church had failed her. That self-proclaiming fountain of love had labelled her a sinner – she, the Catholic party in the relationship, was living in sin, 'And I knew only too well the outcome of that! I was so furious…yet the fight went on within me,' so she had lit the candles to Our Lady and spoken with the nice priest in Hereford, but it had done no good. There was now no all-consuming passion left to which she might subordinate her energies, except perhaps a passion for destruction, self-destruction.

Bit by bit, lying there in her room, she began to peel away the veneer of respectability and seek out the lovelessness inside, identifying and picking over a list of repulsions, headed by Kate coming down on her from a great height, her warm, whisky-soaked breath fouling her nose and throat, that slack mouth of hers grinning at her as it uttered a befuddled 'Give us a kiss.' Or Kate's boyfriend, a young lodger called Mulhattan, who came from

Catherine's drawing of Hereford Cathedral. The printer told her she had the art of texture, of making stone look like stone. It was an art that only a few years later she would apply to environment and character in her novels with similar success.

Birkenhead and sat little Katie on his knee. She was quite used to knees. She would love to sit on her grandparents' knees. One of the reasons why people wanted to lift her on their knees was because she was so small, and pretty of course, too. That day, when she was sitting on Mulhattan's knee, parting his hair and plaiting it, she suddenly noticed there was something about this fella's knee that wasn't quite right… she yelled at him and then he got her in his arms and carried her to a leather chair, where he set about kissing her in a terrible fashion. Stiff and petrified with fear, something bursting inside her, she begged and cried to him to stop, that she knew what he was going to do, and that she would tell her da.

There followed a terrible fight when her granda returned and the man was never seen again, but her drunken mother and the lodger Mulhattan were far from being the only corruptions of love little Katie knew. There was, too, the time when she was repeatedly made to kiss a tobacconist, who kept what was known as a house-window shop, in Lancaster Street. He and his wife mopped up the out-of-hours-custom of the main shop in Philipson Street. Catherine would be sent to get tabs for brother Jack or baccy for old John, maybe late in the evening. The shopkeeper was small and white-haired, a man well into his sixties. After the first time he kissed her, Katie stood in the backlane pressing herself tightly against the wall with her legs tightly crossed and bit into her lip, for the fear in her was making her want to go to the lavatory. She determined never to go to the shop late in the evening again… But needs must, so she got into the habit of holding the door open ready to run, and the man got into the habit of withholding her change until he had what he wanted. Her nightmares were frequent during this period… The business was terminated when the family left the New Buildings in a rush. Why, little Katie never knew nor cared, the relief was so great.

Catherine began to be overwhelmed with feelings of hopelessness, lovelessness, self-loathing and hate. As she put it to me, she began to want to 'wreak retribution on somebody or something, especially for losing the babies.' In *The Garment*, when Grace Rouse is on the edge of mental breakdown she calls to David, her one support, and tells him she no longer likes herself inside, and this was where Catherine's thoughts were leading. She tackles the whole terrifying business of breakdown

Her six-week treatment at St Mary's Psychiatric Hospital, Burghill was the bottom of the pit for Catherine. But there was no instant cure.

in this novel, which it took her three years to write, a very long time by her standards. Afterwards, she gave it to her friend Dr Mannie Anderson to check the material on nervous breakdown from a medical point of view.

The novel is all about the corruption of love. I used to think that the name of the main protagonists, Donald and Grace Rouse, was richly ironic, given that Donald is impotent, but Catherine used names from her past without a thought to character, and I shouldn't have been surprised to find that Annie Rouse was Assistant Superintendent Nurse and Tutor Sister at Harton Institution from 1926.

Driven to the precipice of insanity by her husband, Grace turns to her friend, Dr David Cooper, but it is too late, she is too far down the path; not even he can help. When Catherine turned to Tom he could do nothing to stem the tide either.

One day, after he had returned to camp, Catherine was gripped by a terror she could neither place nor understand. Her heart raced, her limbs trembled, she felt sick and was sure she was going to die. She had been found lying on the bed, stiff, wild-eyed and silent. Later, she would discover that the terror had a name – *nervous hysteria* – but no-one told her that at the time.

In *The Garment*, Grace finally cracks yelling and screaming mouthfuls of abuse. She is restrained on her bed by her husband, who shouts at their son Stephen to fetch 'Uncle David' at once. It's a moment when one

Images of Kate and from her childhood pervaded her nightmares until, like Sarah in The Blind Miller, *she lay helpless, bound to her bed like the timbers of the Slake, sinking, choking in the black mire.*

identifies wholly with the child, the shock of seeing his parents out of control. So often it is a man called David, the name of Catherine's dead child (who might have turned her own world round), who offers succour to her mentally unstable fictional heroines. In *Maggie Rowan*, he discovers Maggie's sister Ann in convulsion before she is taken to the asylum. In *The Blind Miller*, where the narrative returns Sarah Bradley to Catherine's 'locus of self-destruction' – the Jarrow Slake – and she dreams she is dragged into the mud, which fills her mouth, she is choking, wallowing, sinking into the black mire until her husband David allays her fears, hugs and reassures her that it is only a dream.

For Catherine, as for Grace Rouse in *The Garment*, it is no dream and David cannot help. In interview with me she used the same metaphor to describe the moment

of descent as she uses for Grace in the novel – all the self-loathing, bitterness and resentment, all the nameless terrors and dread came to a head, and 'the boil burst'.

Grace becomes almost objective at this point. There is relief at the bursting. Even though she can hear the filth pouring out of her mouth, she manages to adopt a conscious strategy designed to get Donald to release the pressure he is exerting on her. She falls suddenly quiet, and when Donald desists she wrests herself away to the other side of the bed, screaming abuse at him – disjointed sentences, the power of which will not be lost on Donald, or indeed on readers looking for autobiography. For 'Kate' is the butt of Grace's rage, albeit she is not Grace's mother… And then Grace lunges at Donald like a wild animal and tears at his face with her claws.

'When the boil burst and my head made into a whirlpool of terror,' Catherine said to me, 'I knew something had to be done.' It sounded all very rational. Catherine always maintained that it was she who had suggested confinement in St Mary's Psychiatric Hospital, Burghill, that she had been quite willing to go, but this was not the case.

In the original draft of *Our Kate*, she uses the

'boil' metaphor again, and it bursts at the very moment that it is suggested she should see a psychiatrist. Then, when subsequently the psychiatrist suggests that she should go for treatment, fear runs riot.

At Burghill, a psychiatric hospital and a good one, Catherine was subjected to electro-convulsive therapy, ECT, the convulsions so severe that they raised her off the slab. She stayed for six weeks. At one stage she notices the kind priest from Hereford visiting other patients and he cannot believe that she is in there, because up until her confinement she had acted so normally.

In July 1945, after six weeks in Burghill, Catherine returned to The Hurst, scared, scarred, far from stable, and again alone. Tom was not de-mobbed until the following February. The house had been rented by a man who had left chamber pots brim full of urine and skipped without paying the rent. She went to see friends across the road and for some reason ended up sleeping in the basement of their house among the boxes. Tom's mother was appalled to find her there when she came to stay. Tom then took a fortnight's leave to get The Hurst back into shape.

After he left, Catherine once more found herself pregnant, and she had

On her return to The Hurst and the garden she loved, she experienced occasional but significant moments of pure joy in a beneficent Nature, quite new to her and instantly creative.

her third miscarriage (the fourth baby) some time after that.

There followed another major low point, but this time she acted with admirable pragmatism, making herself a chart, a daily record of her fears and how she had in fact coped with them. There wasn't a day in that first year at home when she didn't have fear attacks, panic attacks, and it was many years before she could cross the list off altogether.

To her fears she could now add the fear of going mad, the fear of doctors and the fear of people finding out that she had been confined in a psychiatric hospital (a stigma almost as great in her mind as that of her illegitimacy), and the fear, which would become Sarah Bradley's in *The Blind Miller*, of her 'new superior little world' exploding, in particular the fear of what a small, select circle of Grammar School masters' wives were saying about her now…

She was lonely. She had lost another child. Tom wasn't there. She was on her own. She was suffering the

aftershock of this ECT treatment, and it was hardly surprising that she came nearer than at any other time to ending her life. She had three boxes of sleeping pills, and couldn't stop herself thinking about how nice it would be to go to sleep and never wake up.

Thinking of Tom, and the effect it would have on him, led to a decisive move which brought her one positive step forward in her rehabilitation. She got up out of bed and flushed them all down the lavatory, and in doing so experienced more relief than she had known for years. It was her first positive move, something to help herself, and for a while she felt she could see light at the end of the tunnel.

With this loving concern for Tom came a no less significant poetic awareness of a beneficent spirit in Nature, quite at odds with her earlier resentment at her lot in life. One day, for example, she was sitting at the piano in the drawing room of The Hurst, staring out at the garden when a gust of wind stirred the trees and a shower of leaves swept past the tall windows and were caught in a shaft of white autumn sunlight. She was instantly immersed in a wave of pure joy, 'as swift in passing as the leaves themselves', and composed a song called 'Falling Leaves' in the wake of it.

This sense of a spirit in Nature infusing her being was instanced again seven years later when she was suffering internal bleeding. A voice inside her told her to get up and go into the garden and plunge her hands into the soil. Tom was thunderstruck when he found her, but typically, when she explained, he simply fetched a cushion for her to kneel on. The bleeding ceased and a hysterectomy was avoided.

Then, in 1954, after she and Tom left The Hurst, she singled out a tree in her new garden against which she took to leaning and fancied she felt the pulsating life force surging, empowering and reaching into her and down into the dense undersoil to the tree's farthest roots.

These were significant moments that served to balance her negative, destructive feelings about Nature

Catherine and Tom, together once again at The Hurst after the war, but now sadly aware that they were unlikely ever to have a family. Just as Catherine had been cheated of a mother, now she would herself never become one.

Tom is second from the right in the front row of the staff picture and on the right in the picture below. After the war he was appointed Housemaster of Norman House, which gave Catherine ever more prominent a position to hold down. She did not take to it. The ECT had given her a big dose of reality thinking. In her mind's eye she no longer figured in the cast list of masters wives. Of the functions she had to attend, the most visible was the annual cricket match between

the masters and the boys on the Central Ground. It was the aim of all wives to appear in their best bib and tucker. But Catherine didn't like cricket and she didn't want to go to the match, in fact she considered it a waste of time…

as a hostile force (so prevalent in certain novels, as we will see), and when Tom came back on the scene in the summer of 1946 he made it a priority to encourage her in them.

Shortly after his return, Tom was appointed Master of Norman House at the Grammar School, which gave Catherine ever more prominent a position in the life of the school. She did not take to it. The ECT had given her a big dose of reality thinking. In her mind's eye she no longer figured in the cast list of masters wives in Tom's world.

Years later, Catherine gave me a taste of how it was living the pretence while all the time on the verge of ripping off the mask and giving vent to her real feelings. Among all the various Grammar School functions she had to attend as Tom's wife, one in which she was most visible was the annual cricket match between masters and boys. On that day, all the teachers' wives were expected to appear on parade in their best bib and tucker…

She didn't like cricket and she didn't want to go to the match, in fact she considered it a waste of time. But of course she went. Dressed up to the nines in veiled hat, carrying gloves and bag, she set off down the Queen's Road and

Only total immersion in painting or writing would set her demons aside, and when she began to turn to images of East Jarrow, Tyne Dock and Shields she found that the environment of her childhood was instantly productive of both character and plot. Also, it would serve, in one novel after the other, to keep her problems centre stage and within her power as a writer to control. Ultimately, however, it was a regressive move that denied her the complete freedom from her past that her leaving the North had promised. The novels were short-term therapy that ensured she would never shed her fears or resentful aggression.

'As to how I write the story,' Catherine once said to me. 'I take two, four or six characters and place them in a certain environment and it is the environment that affects their characters. That started, I then find my end. I always think of the end of the story before I begin it. I compare this to going into a station and asking for a single ticket and I'm asked where to? And if I didn't know, then why was I asking for a ticket. So what I do next is to go to the pictures. By this I conjure up every scene and every character in it as if I was looking at a film and I act these characters... No, I don't act them, I become them!'

was just about to cross to the cricket ground when she noticed a brick lying in the gutter and stopped, gripped by a desire to pick the brick up and hurl it through the plate glass window of a nearby Tailor's shop.

On another occasion, she spoke to me about how the loss of her babies had driven her close to snatching one from a pram, worse still of snatching one and throwing it to the ground. It was saying and writing such things that filled Catherine's mail bag in later years with letters from people relieved to find someone willing to share the agonies to which polite society could never admit such a loss could lead, and which doctors ignored or buried out of sight. Catherine said that it was fifteen years after losing her babies before the desire to harm a child was completely under control, and even then she couldn't bear to hold one.

Only total immersion in writing or painting could set her demons aside. Following the incineration of her shorts stories and workhouse sketches, Catherine had returned to the Hurst after her breakdown and begun writing plays, mostly set in an upper class milieu that she thought would be popular. After completing the third play, however, she realised that they weren't working. It isn't clear what actually tipped her into a decision to write about the North. She told me that her reading of Lord Chesterfield's *Letters* had shown her the importance of writing plain, clear English, and that the experience of her breakdown and the ECT had brought her down with a thump to reality. For the first time, she saw herself as she really was, a fugitive. Ever since Aunt Mary had said her father was a toff, she had been running away from her true self. Now she realised that if she was ever going to write a word that anybody would want to read, she'd have to be *herself.*

This return to hard reality was the mood in which a number of short stories about her childhood and then, at length, the first novel (started towards the end of 1946) were written. If you have read *Kate Hannigan*, you will see that realism is what the opening pages are all about. But I wonder whether Tom may have steered her in this direction as a way of getting over her breakdown. In *The Menagerie*, Larry has a breakdown and in the aftermath is steered by Jessie into writing about people he knows, about Aunt Lot, because life *revolves* around Aunt Lot, because Aunt Lot symbolises a whole

way of life. Perhaps Tom tipped her into writing about Kate. It is there in the fiction, where Catherine always put her true feelings.

The problem was that the one person Catherine dared not think about was her mother. In Kate, she earthed all her anguish. As the woman who had conceived her in selfish pleasure, Kate was responsible for the state of mind in which she now found herself. She wrote twice a week. Catherine did not reply. She was finished with Kate. She claimed to have wanted her to die for years, and now she blamed her for bringing her near to madness.

Nevertheless, Catherine determined to write about the people of the North. The decision was a turning point. She dropped her mask, opened the locked doors of her mind and out poured the lives of her people, folk she had rubbed shoulders with for twenty-three years… Once released, they came alive on the page, and she dealt with them by following the instruction of her tutor, Lord Chesterfield, she portrayed them in plain English.

'Tom was de-mobbed in '46,' Catherine recalled for me. 'Soon, he was back at school. I mostly dressed in two dressing gowns, a huge pair of Eskimo-like boots and a big woollen scarf around my head, and worked in that freezing barracks [The Hurst]. It had no central heating of any kind and had only one large fireplace in the drawing room and a number of small ones in other rooms. 'Twas after the war and we were still on coal ration of a ton a year. So I spent at least an hour a day sawing old trees down and sawing them up to keep some kind of warmth in one room… and writing every spare minute. I thought that the only way I could get through the breakdown, which was deep on me, was to write what I knew about, such as my early life.'

With fresh seriousness of intent, she joined the Writers Circle in Hastings, where the youngest member, 19-year-old Joan Moules, remembers, above all, her demand for realism in others' writing: 'Catherine was a brilliant critic... She talked about your story, about the characters, about the setting. Would they have done that? That sort of thing. Realism!'

In this mind set, Catherine denied herself any false props. That, of course, also meant her religion, which she had railed against in the asylum at Burghill.

Now, in 1946, she was determined to put the pieces

Right: Cousin Sarah and Catherine in July, 1946, in the garden of The Hurst. Below: Sarah playing with Tigger, Catherine and Tom's cat.

'I was just educated at an ordinary Catholic school, a very good school, but here I was talking about my religion with Tom, with his MA from Oxford, and Kitty, who was self-educated and very strong in her opinions... Of course Tom was gentle but Kitty was robust, *and I thought, I have got to get out of this house.'*

back together again, albeit in a shape quite different to Catholicism. During this period she read anything medical or philosophical that she could lay her hands on to help sort out her state of mind, and so serious was she that by 1952 she could give a BBC Radio broadcast entitled 'Get Your Nerves Under Control', the fourth of three broadcasts on *Woman's Hour*, which she gave from 1949, a year before her first novel was published.

It is important to appreciate that in Tom, Catherine had found someone with whom she could discuss the small things in life, like death and religion and love, and as she hauled herself out of the nightmare of breakdown, there was intellectual ferment at The Hurst.

Where once Kate had been smearing jam on door handles and she and Nan had been cackling at other of her practical jokes, there was now a liberal intellectual atmosphere. Just how opposed to the general run of things had been any kind of intellectual exploration, pre-Tom, was shown on the night Kate had served mousetrap pie for dinner. To the amusement of Nan and crew at one end of the table, Kate had broken the pie crust to reveal an old pan scourer and rusty mousetrap. Meanwhile, at the other end, Catherine was being introduced to the writing of Voltaire by a French friend. By the time she and Tom decamped for the St Albans flat in 1940, Catherine had built up a reading list, which she went through systematically during the ensuing years and which included, among other authors:

Plutarch, Thomas Carlyle, Smiles, Clarendon, Macaulay, Johnson, Boswell, The Bible, Homer, Virgil, Aesop, Montaigne, Bacon, Dante, Thomas A Kempis, H O Arnold Foster, Seeley [and various early histories], Saxon literature: Caedmon, Bede, Aldhelm, Boethius; Chaucer, Langland, Wyclif, Mandeville,

More, Shakespeare, Milton, Dryden, Steele, Addison, Swift, Goldsmith, Defoe, Fielding, Smollett, Pope, Burns, Cowper, Gilpin, Scott, Coleridge, Wordsworth, Byron, Shelley, Keats, Browning, Rossetti, Tennyson, Austen, Dickens, Thackeray, George Eliot, Lytton, Bronte, Ainsworth, Trollope, Wilkie Collins, Kingsley, Stevenson, Hardy, Kipling, Dumas, Barrie, Conan Doyle, Haggard, Plato, Machiavelli, Rousseau, Darwin, Marx, Freud...

Now, following her breakdown, Catherine was back on a rigorous intellectual and psychological re-examination and the house was abuzz with it. She couldn't bear people who didn't question what was going on around them. She couldn't bear people to be satisfied, content; that was not what life was about, and she could be blunt. In the fray, if she sensed weakness in a person's argument or they failed to stand up and argue their position, she would pounce and not be afraid to tear into them.

Cousin Sarah first visited The Hurst in 1946 at the moment Catherine was sorting herself out, and completely unaware that she had even been in hospital. This young, unquestioning Catholic, Sarah Lavelle, arrived from the pit village of Birtley and was fair knocked sideways by the ferment:

It was a different world altogether. I first met Kitty in 1946 when I had a recurrence of osteomyelitis [a bone marrow disease] and Aunt Kate wrote to her and asked if I could go down to recuperate. It was not long after the breakdown, but I didn't know that at the time. I think I was down there for a month. I had been brought up a very strong Catholic, so she took me to church on Sunday, to Mass – Oh, it was horrendous really! When we came out we met a few people and started to chat, and she said, 'Well it does nothing for me,' and I said, 'Well it's the way I've been brought up.' I was just educated at an ordinary Catholic school, a very good school, but here I was talking about my religion with Tom, with his MA from Oxford, and Kitty, who was self-educated and very strong in her opinions. So they started on about the Catholic Church and all the pomp and everything, which was their point of view and I was trying to put my faith across to them, and I was so upset because I had never had any friction like that before. I had always sat in the corner, being the youngest. Even when Jack first married me he said to me, 'Don't you ever answer back?' (He's sorry he said that now.) They were running my faith down and I was trying to defend my faith as best I could and I found it very difficult. Of course Tom was gentle, but Kitty was *robust,* and I thought I have got to get out of this house. This was the very first weekend I was there! And then I walked in the evening to Benediction and when I got back the wound in my leg opened up, so she said, 'That's what you get for going to church!'

Sarah told me about two people, who were particularly close to Catherine and

Catherine around the time she had her first novel, Kate Hannigan *accepted by Macdonalds for publication.*

'She wasn't published then, but she had a kind of confidence. I think she knew that she ought to become a published writer. She may not have had much education but she was a very intelligent woman, she knew things for certain, though she was far from sure that others would recognise the truth of what she knew.' (Joan Moules)

Tom from this time. She called them humanists, but connected them also with the Unitarian Church – 'a lovely couple, every time I went down to Hastings we saw these people.' Later, I discovered from Tony Weeks-Pearson just how significant a spiritual influence one of them had on Catherine.

Tony, who arrived as a pupil at the Grammar School shortly after the war, also corroborated Sarah's picture of the lively artistic and intellectual nature of the scene at The Hurst, which is lacking in Catherine's own representations of these days.

Kitty was a very sociable person, her health was fairly good then. She was a fencer, a painter, a writer, she was everything really... My great connection with her through the rest of her life was through someone who lived down Hoads Wood Road. Her husband was the pastor, the minister of the Unitarian Church... Denbeigh and Muriel

Hilton. The closeness was not with Denbeigh, nor on Tom's account, really, it was the women. Muriel used to keep in regular telephone contact with Kitty almost throughout their lives. Muriel had a great influence on Kitty, indeed she influenced a lot of people, including the brothers of the Powys family [three writer brothers brought up in the Dorset-Somerset countryside, Llewellyn, Theodore and John Cowper Powys, who wrote *A Glastonbury Romance, Maiden Castle,* etc]. She also knew John Masefield [Poet Laureate from 1930]. Muriel did a monthly column in the Unitarian journal, *The Enquirer,* and people used to write to her from all over the place. She was a nice poet, too. But, with Muriel, the *person* was the message. She was one of the most…what would you say?… You would be *struck* when you went into a room… Dramatic? No, absolutely the opposite, *tranquil*, at peace with herself.

The thing was, I think, that the two women [Catherine and Muriel] were opposites. Hilton exercised a calming influence, a reassurance, at least for a few minutes (which was itself something of a miracle in Kitty's case). The Cooksons lived up the top of Hoads Wood Road and Muriel and Denbeigh lived, until their deaths, down the bottom, so they would meet at bus stops and things.

Having said how calm Muriel was, she also had a tremendous sense of fun, and so close was the relationship that they would burst into laughter spontaneously, like girls, when they saw each other in the distance, which was extraordinary in two women so apparently responsible and mature. Kitty was a great laugher, a very sociable person…

I had the same sort of picture of Catherine from Mannie Anderson, a South Shields doctor, who, as we shall see, became an important friend from the 1950s. He described her as a *cyclic* personality. She could be up one minute and deep down the next, but she was very sociable, great fun, tremendous company, and I think that also gets lost in Catherine's descriptions of herself.

The other spiritual influence, and the man who showed Catherine how she could strip out the dogma and reinterpret Christianity in terms she could more nearly accept, was Leslie D Weatherhead, a pioneer in the integration of psychology and religion. His was a new spin on Christianity, immensely attractive to Catherine because it no longer relied upon the naive terror tactics of Roman Catholicism. She read his book, *The Christian Agnostic*, and identified with the person of the title: 'a person attracted by Christ who seeks to meet the challenges, hardships and sorrows of life in the light of that spirit, but who feels that he cannot honestly and conscientiously "sign on the dotted line" that he believes certain theological ideas about which the Church dogmatises.'

Weatherhead recorded his feelings after a near death experience during a serious operation: 'There was no regret for lost opportunities, no reviewing of life's history, no concern whatever for a reward or punishment, only a strong

Harry Edwards was healing in the theatre on Hastings Pier. Catherine was one of hundreds watching people walk away, their ailments cured.

abiding sense of calmness and peace, and that I was in the hands of an infinitely benign power which cared for me and would protect me from all that was ill; a power whose attributes were goodness and mercy. The whole scheme of life on this earth, death, and the certain life to come, seemed to have meaning and purpose, to be harmonious, natural, and, above all, beneficent.'

With Weatherhead, Catherine could move on from Father O'Malley's vengeful God of the Old Testament. The influence of Weatherhead and Muriel Hilton brought her to an understanding of life that incorporated a metaphysical reality and a morality that was not prescribed by fear. Perhaps it was due to them (and one other, who gave her direct personal experience of the spiritual, meta-physical element) that she did not go the whole hog into humanism.

Around this time she developed a painful sinus below the eye, which her doctor indicated would need an operation. Then, still waiting for the sinus to be seen to, a friend persuaded her to go to a seance at the House of Healing, a well-known Spiritualist Centre in the town. Catherine agreed and was impressed when 'contact' was made with two people she had known – she writes in detail about this in *Let Me Make Myself Plain*. Later, she returned to the centre and received treatment for her sinus. There was a laying on of hands, again the session worked, seemingly miraculously. In *The Maltese Angel*, Stephanie McQueen (who is the Maltese Angel), has the healing gift from her mother and turns it on for the boy, Carl, in circumstances similar to the healing of her sinus.

Catherine herself developed an ability to put Tom to sleep when a migraine threatened, and in the 1980s had the shock of her life when the wife of her solicitor had been brought to their house in a terrible state following a car accident and she had done the same to her. When her husband arrived they hadn't been able to wake her up. Catherine determined never to dabble in the art again.

The art of healing she felt flowed in a line at least as far back as Christ, 'this great healer, this man who understood human nature so well,' as she once described Christ to me. It was one element of the Christian story that she never questioned. Even in The Hurst when she had done with the Church, she still believed 'in the *man* Jesus. I do not believe in the tenets of the Catholic Church or any other sect or religion. You understand me? I believe in *him*, the man, the thinker, the *healer*, the man who recognised the great spirit that was in him, and used it to the extent of dying for his principles… There have been many healers since, such as Harry Edwards,

Joan Longfellow snapped in Hastings in 1950, when she first met Catherine. 'I was very young. I hadn't wanted to read my story, but she didn't let anyone get away with it.'

who I believed in as a healer…'

One day she went along to watch the then famous healer perform a demonstration on Hastings Pier. Catherine was among hundreds in the audience and was astonished as one by one people trooped up to him and he relieved their pain. Even cripples appeared to walk away unaided. She couldn't tell whether he cured them by manipulation or some other means, but what amazed her was the ordinariness of a man apparently capable of miracle after miracle.

As a result, she wrote to Edwards, and there began an association which, though she met him only once, Catherine became convinced facilitated events and solved problems in her life. She ascribed to Edwards the cure in 1953 that obviated the need for a hysterectomy, which I have described. She would let Edwards know when she had a problem and he would give her the confidence to rely on the voice within that he told her is always waiting to be heard. It would seem that even as she was fiercely in opposition to the Church, Edwards gave meaning to an idea that had always confused her, that the Kingdom of God is within.

This was the nature of her spirituality – a power within, capable of resolving and transforming. Far from seeing a contradiction between her drive for realism and this spiritual avowal, the power seemed more accessible in a starkly real environment, as the novels show.

In 1948 a 17-year-old Hastings girl called Joan Longfellow won a short story competition in *Woman's Own* and received a letter from the editor suggesting that she join the Hastings Writers Circle to brush up on her technique. Enclosed was the address of the Secretary, Mrs C Cookson, The Hurst, 81 Hoads Wood Road.

'We weren't on the telephone,' recalls Joan today, 'so I wrote a letter, saying I was interested in writing and could I come along to the Circle, and she wrote back and gave me all the details. She said, I am just finishing as Secretary and the next meeting we are handing over to the new Secretary, come along and I'll introduce you. I went along to the Rougemont Hotel in Harold Place [since demolished], where they used to meet, and hers was the only name I knew.'

This will have been early in 1950. Catherine had been a member of the Circle since 1946, she had by then

Enclosed was the address of the Secretary, Mrs C Cookson, The Hurst, 81 Hoads Wood Road.

written the manuscript of *Kate Hannigan*, her first novel. It had been accepted for publication by Macdonalds, but it would not be published until June. In the meantime, Catherine had submitted her second novel, published only recently as *Kate Hannigan's Girl*. Macdonalds had agreed to publish it, but had expressed reservations about it. In fury she had recalled the manuscript and begun work on *The Fifteen Streets*.

Joan gives us a portrait of Catherine at precisely this time that is different from the one Sarah gives because Joan is not family, on the contrary it is a professional relationship. Joan is embarking on the same literary adventure as Catherine, who shows her best side in encouraging the young woman, and no small degree of compassion:

We sat round on chairs in a half circle with the Chairman and the Treasurer and the Secretary at the top. Someone would read a story and the Chairman would say, 'Let's have some comments, start here,' and they would go round the room. I was very young, 18, 19. I hadn't wanted to read, I think I had gone three weeks without reading and it was Catherine who said to me, 'You've joined a writers circle, you want people to comment on your stories. We can't if we don't hear them.' She didn't let anyone get away with it even though (perhaps because), as I found out later, she had found it difficult herself. So, I plucked up courage to read. I thought if I didn't I'd be thrown out of the circle. I had deliberately picked a very short story so that I wouldn't have to read for long. One by one they more or less all said, 'This is a young writer worth encouraging,' sort of patting me on the head. So it went round, each one making nice little comments, 'lovely little story,' etc. Then it came to Catherine, there was silence for a minute (I'll never forget it) and then she took a deep breath –

I had kept my head down, just looking up when people were making their comments because it is mortifying at first when it happens – and she took a deep breath and said, 'Yes, it's got a lot of potential, but it's *not* a nice little story. It *can* be a nice little story but it isn't yet, you've got work to do on that story.' Then she took it from the beginning (luckily it was only a couple of pages) and she said, 'The start, where you mention so-and-so, you should have done this, and I was listening with my eyes down, feeling quite embarrassed but trying to take it all in, and then she finished with, 'There's a lot of potential, a lot of potential, but I suggest you revise it and bring it back next week and we'll see.' And then we went on to the next story and I sat there letting my blushes go down, and at the end of that meeting, and before reading that story, she came up to me and said, 'You took that *very* well. Would you like to come with us to chocolate? [Members of the Circle would go to Dimarco's, a coffee shop, afterwards.] There are things that I want to say to you, because you have got it in you to become a writer.'

Now, she wasn't published then, but it didn't stop her saying these things, she had a kind of confidence. I think she knew that she, too, ought to become a published writer. She may not have had much education but she was a very intelligent woman, she knew things *for certain*, though she was far from sure that others would recognise the truth of what she knew.

Joan went on to write numerous novels under her married name (Joan Moules) for the publisher, Robert Hale – mysteries, romances and two biographies, and she was writing her first historical novel when we met, as well as running a Writers Circle of her own.

Just as Catherine told members of the Hastings Writers Circle exactly what she thought of what they had written, so she was equally ruthless with herself. Above all else, what she was after was realism. In her crits at the Circle she never touched on the grammar or the construction of sentences. It was the realism of the setting, the characters and the story that mattered to her.

This was the truth serum that Catherine was injecting into her own writing post-1945. So intense was the effect of it off the page that Murray Thompson, the first publisher to read *Kate Hannigan*, wanted to turn the novel down, believing it to be too strong for his market. Fortunately, as everyone now knows, his secretary took the manuscript home, read it overnight and told Murray he *must* accept it.

The amazing thing, however, was the dedication on the front page, which reads: 'To my mother who has found her expression through me'. At the time Catherine wrote the line, she still blamed Kate for her mental breakdown. Kate was writing up to two letters a week to her daughter, and Catherine was not replying to them.

By 1950, however, they *were* corresponding. Her mother was working for a Dr Carstairs in South Shields. Kate writes, revealing her simple, straightforward nature, from 352 Alice Street –

The Dr. gets Books from some library and he came in yesterday with KH [Kate Hannigan], he was bucked up, & called me in to tell me, well, Mrs (indecipherable) Read it, and she said this morning, yes she said it was very [underlined] interesting, & would be nice for people that belonged the north, but why not more cheery subject, & I told her that the publishers did not want that. They wanted Books of the same type, not dribble *[sic]* & then she said, Kitty is a very clever woman, like her mother. I said, I am very sorry, but I [underlined twice] have no money, so please no complements *[sic]*. Dr. did laugh. She is very weak but her Real worry is this Blasted Home, yes lass send any letters on any thing, to Drs until I tell you otherwise & so lass time is flying it is now 9.30 & the weather has been awful. Slush and sleet but I get a tram each morning when it is like this.

All my love to you Both
& god Bless you
Health & happiness

Your affec
Mother
xxxx

Going to hurry now
Cheerio

There followed four sheets of paper containing all sorts of factual information that Catherine had requested about living in East Jarrow and Shields in the early years of the 20th century. So, Catherine was using her mother as a vital research resource, but was that the only sense in which Kate was achieving her expression through the novels?

The answer, of course, is no. Yet, the realism on which Catherine was insisting did not extend to an injection of Kate's real character in the novels. She still could not face that. Kate Hannigan may seem to us to be Kate Fawcett, Catherine's mother, because her illegitimate daughter, Annie, seems to be Catherine, doing all sorts of things that we know Catherine did when she was a child, and her parents Tim and Sarah seem to be John and Rose, but in fact there is no character in any of the novels that is Kate, either as she saw her mother or as

Catherine with Kate in 1954. She had built her mythology of the North around her, but now, suddenly, the real Kate was lying in the bedroom upstairs.

others saw her. The psychological trick that Catherine was pulling was not to write about her mother as a person, or even any longer to consider her as such in real life, but to *transform her into a symbol*.

We have all these facts in the novels, particularly in the early ones, facts which equate to facts of Catherine's childhood, and so we imagine that all she is doing is giving us her childhood in readable story form. But these facts – the fetching of the beer, the going to the pawn, all the things in the novels which I mentioned in my early chapters as true to life – are events in a mythology, which, like Greek myth, is not in essence true-life history. Greek myth deals with the political and religious history of the Aegean, but it deals with it in an imaginative way, poeticising it in order to make points relevant to all people and all ages. Similarly, even though Catherine's early novels deal with her personal history, their purpose is not to record events like documentary, but to unearth the heroic/tragic image of Northern culture 'that comes from way back and threads the people of this particular area,' as Catherine once put it to me.

Kate appears in many of the novels, as she does in the first novel as Kate Hannigan, not dishing out sweets at the door in exchange for potato peelings, as Winnie remembers her, nor as the harridan Catherine remembers, forcing

Kate, terminally ill, dozing by the front door of Loreto, the house where Catherine and Tom took her in 1954.

her daughter to suffer the indignity of taking John's trousers to the pawn, but as a mythic figure or symbol of something deep in the subconscious of Tyneside people, as 'a symbol of earth, of home, of blood, of race…of the deepest ground from which life emerges and to which it returns.'

In the first novel, Rodney Prince sees this in Kate Hannigan. He realises that it has to do with the reason why he has decided to come and work among the Tyneside poor. When finally he and Kate come together it is a celebration of that same something.

There is very often a figure in the novels who performs this function, a woman in touch with the spirit of Tyneside – every instinctual female figure (often, but not always, called Kate) from Kate Hannigan through Lally Briggs in *Pure as the Lily* (a sheer expression of 'wisdom without learning', the very hallmark of working class culture) up to Kate Makepeace in *Dinner of Herbs* (a personification of the harsh lead mining Northumberland countryside, out of which Catherine's people came).

On the face of it, it is extraordinary that Catherine should choose the woman she claimed she hated more than any other, and whom she blamed for the agonies of her mental breakdown, to put at the fulcrum of her books in this way. But Kate was the obvious candidate. She was Catherine's mother, she was the root of Catherine's problems *and* her needs.

What's more, Kate had always signified something special, which had nothing to do with the fact that she was her natural mother. When Kate was nowhere near, Catherine would remember the moments when her mother seemed to have a line into the spirit of East Jarrow, like the time when, quite sober, Kate had spontaneously seized Catherine's hand and run along the bank of the Tyne, chasing the clouds as they scudded over the moon, before collapsing into her daughter's arms, laughing fit to burst, or when Kate and other women of the New Buildings would dress up as men and go beating the bounds, as had been done on the Tyne since time immemorial.

Kate's instinctual nature meant that she *was* her environment in a way that Catherine, with all her desire to uproot, could never be. Kate was warm, unaffected, generous, simple, straightforward, and that telling phrase, wise without learning.

In Kate the lines of communication were open to poetic truth in a way they never were to the daughter, and perhaps there lay Catherine's real, subconscious regret of the mix-up that stole her mother from her at birth. With the enforced separation she was cut her off from her true fount of inspiration.

Now, following her breakdown, Catherine's need was to write and to get back to the fount. As for Jimmy in *Pure as the Lily* – her need went beyond the desires of the torturous days of childhood, beyond the rejections that had been heaped on her and she had heaped on others, beyond the self-recrimination, beyond this past life into something only dimly comprehended, but well-deep, and her birthright. Jimmy found the answer to his need in warm, unaffected, generous, simple, straightforward Lally, who, like Kate, was wise without learning. Henceforth, there wouldn't be a day or a night when Jimmy and Lally were apart, and now the same would be true, in an imaginative sense, of Catherine and Kate.

Catherine was coming to terms with the fact that Kate *belonged* to the East Jarrow community in a way that she never had. When she thought of Kate, now that she was back home and Catherine was renewing her acquaintance imaginatively with people she had not seen for twenty years, it seemed that her mother embodied the spirit of her community, and Catherine knew that she needed to draw on that. She needed to come home, to the home that Kate knew, to the mother she had always refused to know.

If she hadn't done so, she would never have come to write the novels that she did. Years later, she would acknowledge to Tyne Tees Television the debt that she owed her mother in this, giving her mother credit for that side of her that enabled her to write and to be 'a little bit of a poet'. This seemed like an amazing advance, certainly it was for the fiction, but to consider that she might owe her mother a debt, when she had always imagined that her talents sprang from her 'gentleman' father, was an extraordinary turnaround.

Kate in her early twenties, not long before Catherine was born. Kate was warm, unaffected, generous, simple, straightforward – wise without learning. In Kate the lines of communication were open to poetic truth in a way they never were to the daughter. But what did it matter now, for Catherine had the imagination to deliver it to her readers. In that sense she enabled a partnership between mother and daughter in her fiction that had not been possible in real life.

Perhaps Catherine's awareness that she lacked this intuitional, loving aspect of Kate, which time and again resolves fractured lives in the novels, did lie among the roots of the hate she felt for her mother. Certainly, envy is often a key emotion. But what did it matter now, for Catherine had the imagination to deliver it to her readers. In that sense she enabled a partnership between mother and daughter in her fiction that had not been possible in real life. They came together in a way they never had before.

That it was a coming together in the realm of the imagination and wasn't real occurred to her one morning in 1953 when a letter arrived at The Hurst from Aunt Sarah.

Sarah had been forced to take responsibility for Kate, but Catherine's real mother was now drinking herself to death and had developed stomach cancer. 'The doctor told her that Kate didn't have very long,' Sarah's youngest told me, 'and my mother wrote to Kitty, and Kitty didn't want to know, she didn't want to come up and get her.'

Catherine couldn't face the reality, but Sarah insisted that Catherine do so, and suddenly the real Kate was lying in the bedroom upstairs.

Except she wasn't, for the real Kate had ceased to exist for Catherine. She found that her perception of her mother had changed since she had translated her into this symbol, she no longer hated her, she even allowed her to drink whisky! In fact, having re-created Kate in fiction, Catherine found that she wanted to be with her mother and talk and, for the first time, listen to what she had to say.

The experience kept Kate alive for three years. She died on September 23, 1956, by which time they had all three moved from The Hurst to Loreto on nearby St Helen's Park Road. After she died, Catherine moved her writing desk into the ground floor room where her mother had passed the last months of her life, the roses 'tapping at the window' from the flower bed outside.

Now she would write with her mother's presence all about her.

Kate on her deathbed, the roses 'tapping at the window' from the flower bed outside.

8 HAPPY FAMILIES

Only Tom knew the depths to which Catherine had sunk in her mental anguish. Just how seriously he held her condition during the war can be seen by his decision, included in Catherine's diary, to embrace Catholicism, to pray to Our Lady for her. This will have been a huge decision for Tom, who didn't care for the Church. But Tom only ever wanted what Catherine needed.

One of the ways he set about trying to help her now was by bringing the energies of his relationships with his pupils back into The Hurst. 'Tom took students in,' recalls Cousin Sarah, 'not paying students, just lads he wanted to help who were at the school. They had a lad called Gub and another lad, there was always someone. They looked after their education in the evening. They didn't stay over, but Tom would do so many hours in the evening with them. So, there was always a lot going on.'

In 1946 Tom became the third ASM of the school's Scout Troop, which clearly was no ordinary scouting organisation. 'That troop was as vital an influence on us as the school itself,' remembers Tony. 'It was a school troop run by a very good parcel

Tom at camp: 'We went further afield in the summer, for the long camp… Kitty was a good painter and would come to camps. I remember making her an easel out of the forest wood, branches and stuff. And of course she was a very sociable person, her health was fairly good then and she was about to launch herself.' Tony Weeks-Pearson

of men, the chief of which was the deputy head, L H G Baker. 'Cookie' [Tom's nickname], like the rest, were assistants to 'Com' Baker. Baker actually had two nicknames, one a school one and one a scout one, which is indicative of the place. 'Strube' was his school nickname, after the cartoonist. He was a Maths teacher as well of course. 'Com' was short for Commodore. They had these naval titles, not sure why. There was a Coxon and a Boson. I don't remember Cookie having one, but he probably did. That troop won all the competitions. And they did this elaborate scout pantomime annually. Kitty was a good painter and would come to camps. I remember making her an easel out of the forest wood, branches and stuff.'

Tom's pupils became their family, and the one family element in Catherine's memories of East Jarrow – New Year's Eve, when ships' horns, dock hooters and church bells all rang out simultaneously, was revived in their drawing room. Tony remembers one occasion in particular: 'We must have been sixthformers at the time

and were invited up to the house. We all had a special relationship through scouts, either troop or patrol leaders. The big thing that I remember, apart from the fact that I took a girl with me, was that Kitty made sure that I was the one to perform "the first footing", I brought in the piece of coal. I remember Cookie – we saw the man in a new light that night. At a certain stage in the evening he took hold of my girlfriend who was a keen dancer, probably did it to make her feel at home because she wasn't anything to do with the school. She was a ballroom dancer and they did the Apache, it was French, a kind of wife-beating drama performed in a sleazy, low Parisienne, Tango style, chucking the woman across the floor… The Hurst was a very handsome house at the top of Hoads Wood Road. They took the carpets up and Cookie had his shoes off and I remember him slipping and going for a burton right across this floor and into the wall…in a very graceful, slow way, no side about him of course.'

Such events were the mainspring of what Tom was trying to create for Catherine at The Hurst. As her readers know, Christmas and New Year are always moments of quiet expectation in the novels, when the tussle of life is suspended and hearts are opened. Catherine's first novel is built around successive

The Cam at Stretham, where Tom continued to introduce Catherine to his outward bound ethos after sampling the Norfolk Broads. His plan seemed doomed to failure. She didn't like water or boats, couldn't swim and had unhappy memories of her sojourn in East Anglia.

Christmas Eves; it is a clever device that has us share this warm feeling of expectation.

Then came Bill, the child they thought they would never have. Not Tom's doing, a present from a friend who had been trying to find a place him for his owner. Like Tom and Catherine's own children, Bill, a Staffordshire Brindle bull terrier, was nearly taken away just as soon as he arrived. Cruelly, after Catherine had fallen in love with the animal, the original owner changed his mind and turned up to retrieve him. Later, however, Bill was returned and there began a relationship that tells us a lot about Catherine's potential for love. Bill wasn't easy, but he had character. He tore their furniture apart and attacked other dogs whenever they came within striking distance, yet, for all that, and unable to control him, Catherine adored him, even after he contracted mange and she caught the disease from him and Tom had to paint her head to foot with a balm to get rid of it.

Catherine's feelings for Bill are shared in Willie Macintyre's relationship with his bull terrier (also called Bill) in *The Menagerie*. The true Bill is, however, kept for *Hamilton*. I have it from Catherine that the following anecdote in the novel happened exactly as she described it. Bill's gait, the 'dot-and-

Catherine at the helm of a hired boat in the summer of 1954, two years before they bought The Mary Ann Shaughnessy.

carry-three step,' a phrase which surely came from the mathematician in the family, resulted from wearing a plaster cast. Bill is but one of many elements in the novel which, in spite of its richly comic vein, challenge the veracity of Catherine's Author Note, in which she states that *Hamilton* is not meant to be another autobiography.

Besides real-life incidents and relationships, and feelings that belong to the period during which Kate and Nan were giving Catherine a hard time in The Hurst, there are also reverberations of this later, happier period with Tom and the thrill she has in being inspired to write. Also, many facts in the life of Maisie Rochester, her central character, encourage us to identify her with her creator. She holds the purse strings in her marriage to Howard Stickle. She owns the house in which they live. She also has a still-born baby due to her rhesus negative blood type, joins a Writer's Circle and becomes a novelist, and, most particularly, she acquires this stray bull terrier, whom she calls Bill, adopting him after he has been injured by a lorry.

With Bill's leg just out of plaster, Maisie takes her new acquisition for a walk. The dog goes along gingerly at first with this uneven gait, even though his cast has now been removed. Then, suddenly, he stops, turns around, looks at his rear leg, stretches the limb out back with all the tension-relieving poise of an athlete about to enter a race, and tears off.

In fact, it seems that this immensely strong hound would quite regularly pull Catherine off her feet and she would hang on for dear life as she sailed through the slipstream behind him. Or, to the wonderment of passers-by, who

Bill, the Staffordshire Brindle bull terrier. 'What do you feed him on?' said the butcher.

could see no dog, she would race off after him after he had slipped his collar and disappeared up snickets and down alleyways in Hastings Old Town.

On this occasion, Bill, having torn off as it were in pursuit of a rabbit, comes to a halt at a quayside lamp post, reeling Maisie in and winding the lead around the post in search of the best place to leave his mark. At that precise moment, a boatman, who has viewed the whole scene, approaches up a nearby gang plank, guffawing with laughter.

Maisie attempts to disentangle the lead, chastising her charge, as the man idly wonders why anyone should pay to go to the pictures when you can get better on the waterfront for free. Maisie's problem is how to get Bill away before he can embarrass her in front of this unwanted audience by sending a torrent of pee down the lamp post between them. She tugs and tugs at the lead, spinning around the post, but Bill walks the opposite way ensuring he is more tightly attached than before. Then, just as she gives one last great tug, he slips his collar, the man makes a lunge for him and the dog is gone – back in the direction they had just come.

With the man's laughter ringing in her ears, Maisie stops for nothing, pounding after him, as Bill, now way ahead, disappears around a corner into the main street. When Maisie arrives at the corner she looks one way up an empty street and then the other…and sees nothing, no sign of Bill at all. Then she remembers the butcher, hurls herself up the street and arrives at the shop door, gasping for air.

Leaning against the doorpost for support she casts her eyes around the shop to find three customers withdrawing cagily, and Bill sitting on the saw-dust floor, looking expectantly up at the butcher. It is the beginning of a new

Whatever Catherine and Bill's feelings about rivers, locks and and boats, having her hand on the tiller was a position Catherine came to enjoy not only in the boating context.

and important relationship. When Maisie goes over to slip Bill's collar over his big ugly head, the dog moves not a whisker, for he can see that the butcher is already in the process of finding him a pound's worth of scraps.

The episode would hardly be worth mentioning in a biography were it not that Bill was such an important element in Catherine's rehabilitation. He appears also in *Rosie and the River*, *Bill and the Mary Ann Shaughnessy* and in *Mary Ann and Bill*. In all of these we get a clear idea of the atmosphere of simple, gentle happiness that Tom was generating for Catherine throughout the 1950s, an atmosphere in striking contrast to one that favoured taking hold of a baby and dashing it to the ground.

Catherine had a love of dogs and subsequent pets also went far to diminish the pain of her inability to have a family. After Bill came a labrador called Simon and then a poodle called Sandy, followed by a bedraggled Shelter poodle, called Sue, which she brought back to normality.

Catherine liked the rascal in Bill and the urchin in Sue, and it is not difficult to see why. The pity was that a novel like *Rosie and the River* should languish on the shelf for many years, unwanted by Macdonalds, because, for her own health's sake, Catherine needed to write these more life-loving novels, and the success of the *Mary Ann Shaughnessy* series and her *Hamilton* trilogy showed that her audience liked to play the full range of what her imagination had to offer, too.

Despite its title, *Bill and the Mary Ann Shaughnessy* is not part of the *MAS* series. It is the last of Catherine's books for children. Mary Ann Shaughnessy is, in this instance, not a little girl but a boat.

Below: The mooring by The Royal Oak Hotel, or the Lazy Otter as it was when Tom rehearsed Catherine in the simple pleasures of Rosie and the River, *an environment he hoped would nurture her creative, unifying, loving side.*

From early in the decade, Tom persuaded Catherine to go on holiday to the Norfolk Broads. It was an attempt to get her away from the Hurst, to escape the gruelling schedule she set herself of ten to twelve hours a day, immersed in her fiction. She claimed to hate the water, but *Rosie and the River* suggests that all tensions flew away when she was on it.

In the novel, Tom and Catherine are recognisably Fred and Sally Carpenter. Like Catherine, Sally hies from Shields, is six years older than her husband, claims not to like boats and cannot swim. Like Tom, Fred Carpenter is five feet five inches small, boat mad and a teacher at Hastings Grammar School, where, as at the real school, the song is 'Sons of William Parker', owing to its foundation in 1878 out of a merger of The William Parker School and one other school.

Also in tune with reality, Sally is conscious of schoolmaster Fred's small, boy-like stature, while Fred appears to use it to advantage and is a real Jekyll and Hyde character, so that Sally never quite knows what to expect – the cheerful, boyish personality or the firm, self-disciplined schoolmaster. A youthful unpredictability

characterises their relationship. It was written just a few years before Catherine became successful, just a little while before Tom slipped under Catherine's iron-willed control.

What we share is a jousting *esprit*. The diminutive Fred, who is plucked straight out of Tom's boy-scout culture and is set, at all costs, on realising his dream of their adventure on the Broads, is stocking up on victuals, which cost-conscious Sally notes they can ill afford. There is a light-hearted, good-humoured spat in the shop close to the shore, badinage following Tom's playfully patting her bottom, and a general feeling of *bonhomie*, a welcome change to the intensity of Catherine's inner life.

She, unlike her husband, is poorly prepared for the outward bound life they are adopting. When he criticises her floral hat as the only one evident in Oulton, she responds by saying the other women look 'like female stowaways in a Robert Louis Stevenson novel'. Then, at the very moment that they are weighed down with boxes and bags of food, Bill turns up threatening to engage in combat with another bull terrier which is softly padding towards them – it is all just exactly what Catherine needs.

So the holiday goes on, the Carpenters befriending 15-year-old Rosie, who gives the novel its title, their relationship like parents and daughter as they help sort out her problems, just as Tom and Catherine loved to do at the Hurst with Tom's pupils, or with Cousin Sarah or Joan Longfellow or Cousin Teri.

The holiday may have been in 1954. The photograph on page 136, showing Catherine sailing, is of that date. Two years later, with the proceeds from the film, *Jacqueline*, based on the first novel in the *MAS* series, *A Grand Man,* they bought their own boat and christened her The Mary Ann Shaughnessy.

Over a period of ten years they holidayed on her, Catherine always, but not seriously, refusing to admit that she was enjoying herself, though it is true that at this stage (and until they came to own their own swimming pool) she could not swim. In the Foreword to *Bill and the Mary Ann Shaughnessy* she tells us that all the incidents in the book did actually happen 'to some extent, except meeting the baddies.'

I have it from family friend Mannie Anderson that

the boat was bought at auction in Blyth, a coastal town to the north east of Newcastle. It was a twenty-six foot cabin cruiser, coloured white up to the super-structure, which was brown with a cream roof, and to Catherine's delight, 'the wheel was very much like that of a car steering wheel.' She fell in love with the craft, and was distraught to discover that 'by the time she got to the auction,' as Mannie recalls, 'a bid had already been accepted.' That night, however, Catherine had a dream that if she took her rosary and put it in a box on board, it would be hers the next day. She did, the bid fell through and she got the boat. Besides anything else, the story shows that for all her bravado at walking out on the Church she was still sufficiently involved to carry a rosary with her when travelling.

Mannie, his wife Rita, and two daughters, Sylvia and Marian – 'those two pairs of lovely legs,' as Catherine referred to them – holidayed with Catherine and Tom on the Mary Ann Shaughnessy, on the Cam at Stretham, close to Soham, which is deep fen country – 'everyone interrelated and deeply suspect,' according to

a boatman that I met down there.

These holidays also produced her novel *The Fen Tiger*, in which her preoccupation is the deep-down character of a people who once lived by spearing fish among the reeds and fiercely defended their watery land from those who would drain it, and their spirit out of them. The novel *Slinky Jane* also owes a debt to these holidays. In the fens, slinky Janes are eels, the catching of them had been described to her one day by an old fisherman.

The hotel where Catherine, Tom and Bill stayed is now called The Lazy Otter, but was then The Royal Oak Hotel. Mannie and his family stayed at a pub nearby called The Green Man, with a permanently drunken goose called Nicholas. It is now a private house.

During one holiday, probably in 1957, Mannie was asked by Catherine to draw up a list of ladies lavatories in the Shields area by way of research for her novel *Fanny McBride* (the heroine, you may recall, becomes a lavatory attendant). 'Forty years of friendship and what have I got to show for it?' laughs Mannie today, 'a book dedicated to me about a ladies lavatory attendant!'

In fact, as Catherine told me, the novel was

Above, left and right, The Mary Ann Shaughnessy, bought after Catherine left her rosary in a box on board.

inspired by him. 'I used to stay at his home when I came up to give talks,' she said, 'and he would get up in the middle of the night if any of the old girls were dying, and he would go to them and comfort them. I thought that was simply marvellous. He told me that one of the saddest things was on visiting day to go into the ward in the hospital and see patients sitting there just staring into space with no visitors even though some of them had big families. This image stayed with me and touched a strong spring in myself, because I have always been lonely... Kitty was born lonely, and that day he told me about those women in the ward I immediately understood what they were feeling, and I had to bring this out. In *Fanny McBride* this *is* brought out. The whole family stay away, except for this one man, we call him Philip, who she didn't like because he was an upstart.'

9 A Beggar On Horseback

'A woman in an old coat and slippers slinking along to the corner shop early in the morning for two ounces of tea… Oh, there were dozens of Fanny McBrides.'

The image of Mannie's patients staring into space stayed with her and she brought it back to self, back to her own loneliness as a child in East Jarrow, infusing Fanny McBride with it. I once asked her, did she know any Fannys? 'Oh, my,' she replied, 'in my early days, in any poor quarter of Jarrow you would see a woman in an old coat and slippers slinking along to the corner shop early in the morning for two ounces of tea, half a pound of sugar and a half pound of streaky bacon, or something along those lines. Oh, there were dozens of Fannys. And Mrs Flannigans? Oh, yes. In any community you'd find a Mrs F, and the Mrs Flannigan who lived opposite Fanny in that book wasn't a patch on my Aunt Mary, the youngest of three sisters, Kate being the middle one, Sarah the elder…'

The novels were Catherine's umbilical cord into the womb of her people, and when her publishing schedule gathered pace in the 1950s and '60s, she began to enjoy the equilibrium they brought her. The novels put her thoughts and feelings centre stage and she guarded jealously her right to develop her own Tyneside mythology, not only in order to delineate the heroic/tragic character of her people, but to improve her own-self-image, so distorted in breakdown.

In support of the fiction there grew up a frequently repeated, catalogue of anecdotes, including some stories that proved too sentimental to stay the distance.

For example, she told Tyne Tees Television that one night she was sleeping in the dess bed with our Kate, when she was awoken by the sound of men singing a song. She couldn't hear the words of the song, but the tune wafted to her on the breeze. It was apparently the tune of *Oft in the stilly night...*

Oft in the stilly night,
E'er slumber's chain has bound me,
Fond mem'ry brings the light
Of other days around me:
The smiles and tears
Of boyhood's years
The worlds of love then spoken
The eyes that shone
Now dimmed and gone
The cheerful hearts now broken.
When I remember all the friends
So link'd together
I've seen around me fall
Like leaves in wintry weather,
I feel like one
Who treads alone
Some banquet-hall deserted
Whose lights are fled
Whose garlands dead
And all but he departed.
Thus oft in the stilly night.

She said that she lay there and cried, that this was her first realisation of compassion for her people, because those men going to Jarrow in the dead of night would be empty bellied. They had no hope, Jarrow was dead. It was from that moment, she said, that she knew that she'd have to get away from the North.

This had nothing to do with why Catherine left the North *in fact*, nor did it fit the very un-romantic myth that she was creating. It was, however, a useful TV cue for a nostalgic interlude by a Northeastern male voice choir, and she used a version of it in *Colour Blind*, her third published novel. But later, when she was ready to get to grips with her real reasons for moving south, and began to work out her own psychology in the novels, the story was dropped from her anecdotal repertoire and not mentioned again.

A detail from J M W Turner's 'Keelmen Heaving in Coals by Moonlight'. Turner rowed onto the Tyne at Jarrow Staithes to make his sketches. The relationship between the finished painting and the real scene is similar to the one between Catherine's mythology of the North and the reality lived. The artist's purpose, in both cases, went further than documentary. Ultimately, in Catherine's case, the novels became the means by which she sought to address the lovelessness of her childhood and youth.

Mannie Anderson, who was then Consultant Physician at the Ingham Infirmary in South Shields, was witness to this process of the imaginative re-creation of Kate's world by her daughter: 'It must have been in

1952 that I invited her to give the presidential address to the Writers Circle in Shields and so began the habit of Tom and Catherine staying with us whenever they were in the area. She wanted to try her speech out on us first. She had only a few notes, a list of dates on a tiny piece of paper and she delivered it fluently, an emotive piece about her early life, ending with the words, "Thank you Kate for giving me life." All three of us were in tears, and the following day the audience at the Town Hall were also in tears. She then returned to our home and repeated it *verbatim* (!) into a tape recorder.'

Mannie and his wife, Rita, and Catherine – all three of them were in tears. So important did her mythology of the North become to Catherine that she struck off anybody who didn't fall in line with it. When Tom's parents were made to listen to the tape as visitors to the Hurst, 'They listened to it all through, sitting next to one another on the couch – that is what Catherine told me,' Mannie said to me, 'but they couldn't see it – eyes down, blank expressions.' They were not moved at all. Pretty soon, they were no longer on the Hurst invitation list. 'If Kitty was against someone, they couldn't get back,' said Rosemary Barker, 'it was very, very difficult.'

Everything was being brought back to self, as Mannie himself soon discovered. With Catherine's permission, he had written a manuscript based on taped conversations with her and made a contract with David & Charles to publish it. But when Catherine read the transcripts she refused to countenance that she had said what indeed she had said. As a friend, Mannie withdrew the manuscript, cancelled the contract and returned his royalty advance. It still lies unpublished to this day.

She was constructing a reality in which she could dwell and be in control in a way she had never been allowed to as a child. She wanted her hand alone on the tiller, as she had years before on Reny's boat, and now she had got it. She must have been aware of what she was doing because she became fascinated with the difference between truth (as opposed to falsehood) and what the writer understands by 'true', which (like an arrow running true) gets to the heart of the matter, and can just as well reside in an untruth or fiction. Her mythology would enable her to deliver this artistic truth, inspire the spirit of the North, and enable transitory peace of mind, but it would not always tally with the way it was – for example, none of the characters who represent her as a child in East Jarrow reject their own people, as she did, and this would inhibit the novels' therapeutic value for their creator.

In *Maggie Rowan* (1954), her fifth novel, Catherine more nearly confronts autobiographical truth, tipping headlong into the real world perhaps too far for fiction. Maggie *is* Catherine. She is rejected by her childhood friends, she despises her own people, she has Catherine's sexual problems, there is Nan's cruelty to Tom, there is the nervous breakdown and an unrealised desire to have children, plus the difficulty Catherine was having at the time in handling other people's children. There are signs in this novel of serious psychological disturbance, as Maggie becomes an artist in resentment and hate, and we should not be surprised that in the next one, Catherine switched tack.

The steep-sided front garden of Loreto, the secluded house where, from 1954, Catherine's imagination took flight.

Catherine told the story that Loreto had been owned by a Miss Harrison, one of three daughters of a millionaire, who had built it after the family split up over 'a question of religion. The three daughters turned Catholic... It was beautifully built. She had had the bricks handmade and the pointing was an art in itself. The woman had something wrong with her skin and, as I understand it, had to wear a mask.' One of Miss Harrison's nurses had received the house as a bequest on her death. This nurse then sold it to Catherine. 'I knew I wanted it straight away. I knew immediately what I wanted to do with it.'

A Grand Man introduces Mary Ann Shaughnessy, a wholly mythic representation of Catherine as a child, and lo and behold the issue that taxes her is the notion that there is an important difference between lying and making up stories. Mary Ann, the storyteller, is saying that on one level fiction may lie, but on a deeper level it distils truths which escape accurate documentary.

She had not yet had a book accepted for paperback publication (that would be *Rooney* to coincide with the film in 1958). Sales had been largely to libraries and only in hardback. However, things began to look up in 1954, when J Arthur Rank took out an option to make a film of *A Grand Man* (later made as *Jacqueline*). In November of that year, Tom and Catherine gave up their battle to keep the Hurst from crumbling and moved less than a mile away to Loreto. Built in 1936 in a steep hollow, and with a large garden and maze of walks through shrubs and trees, fashioned by Tom over the ensuing years. Loreto's very topography offered greater seclusion for Catherine to concentrate on developing her life out of her fiction, now so imaginatively intertwined.

Just as Kate had been bound into the project as facilitator, so now Tom also found himself ever more at Catherine's beck and call, even though he would shortly take on additional duties at the school as Senior Maths Master.

As facilitators like Lily Maguire had discovered before him, Tom found that this involved some testing abuse, though it must surely have puzzled him when he read the manuscript of *The Blind Miller*.

The Blind Miller is one of Catherine's 'social histories'. Set in the 1930s, its socio-historical perspective is that of the Jarrow March, and, as ever, Catherine meets it with her own crusade, shifting the ground from worker exploitation by the capitalist bosses to the ignorance, prejudice and hypocrisy which she felt kept her people down, and at the same time showing them the way out of their self-made prison to freedom down a path of truth – giving themselves to what the strongest of them knew in their hearts to be true, giving themselves uninhibitedly to their intuition.

It is an extraordinary book from an autobiographical point of view. In it, the Kate myth of Northernness reaches a new level of development, gathering a kind of primitive authenticity, which has relevance way beyond the bounds of Tyneside in which the story is set. One feels that if she had had the wisdom of it at the time she first left the North there would have been no going back, no taking Kate back, and probably no marriage to Tom either, because with this wisdom she would no longer have needed the kind of strength Tom gave her. This is why it reads like an assault on Tom.

In his efforts to rescue her from the brink of madness he had brought not only his kindness and gentleness and good humour to bear, but also the approach of the mathematician and his knowledge of Latin, giving her lessons in grammar and punctuation, which unfortunately served to stultify her free prose. While she was worrying about Tom's syntactical rules, she was losing the spontaneity of her writing, she was losing the 'connection', an intuitional rapport, which had, for example, enabled her to voice the complete story of *The Fifteen Streets* in one go, all of a piece, and which she had seen working its miracles in another context at the House of Healing in Hastings.

There is precedent for this in literature. The 19th-century ploughman poet and prose writer John Clare had eschewed formal rules and punctuation for the same reason. Unfortunately, in Catherine's case, the tussle over syntax with Tom showed that they were not, in this at least, on the same wavelength at all. It put him in a category that excluded him from the inner sanctum, where she felt in touch, through Kate, with that thread that linked her with the spirit of her people.

'On their skill and their toil has been built England's industrial revolution. They were crowded into hovels, their children starved and died, and on their sacrifice great capital has been accumulated.' So wrote Ellen Wilkinson about the unemployed workers who marched on London in 1936. Catherine's novel, The Blind Miller *was set around the famous march and may be said to sculpt working class society of the time with more realism, but its main purpose is to give wings to her mythology of the North, where the truest characters are their own environment, primitive, uncultivated, animistic… while the well-educated, good and the kind (one of whom is identified with her husband, Tom) are relegated to the fringes. Her God is a blind, uncaring version of Longfellow's miller, who 'grinds us all'.*

She spells this out, somewhat cruelly, in this novel, linking the animistic force that inspires to the primitive animalistic energies of uninhibited sex, from both of which the 'Tom' character in this fiction is excluded.

There are two kinds of sex in the novels, 'married or respectable sex' and 'spontaneous sex'. The first kind is weighed down with mutual respect and fertility symbols, often involving the cupping of a breast in the palm of the man's hand. The second is sex in response to a violent force beyond the control of the protagonists, an exciting, primitive, animalistic passion, aligned with a different symbolism of the very force that empowers.

In *The Blind Miller* we have both kinds, and Catherine is freeing her heroine to enjoy the latter, as if

David and Tom are left out in the cold. They are not authentic, they do not understand... There couldn't have been a more complete disposal of Tom, except by the means she chose to dispose of David in the novel – she blows him up with a bomb!

responding to an all-inspiring primitive force within.

She wrote the novel after nearly twenty years of marriage to Tom, and possibly ten years before Nan, on her deathbed, gave him the letters which, according to Catherine herself, destroyed her moral reputation in his eyes. Nan had saved the letters, you will recall, with one purpose in mind, finally to break up Tom and Catherine's relationship.

Like Catherine and Tom, the main protagonists in *The Blind Miller*, Sarah Bradley and David Hetherington, are Catholic and Protestant respectively. Sarah's father has already flayed her sister, Phyllis, alive for consorting with an Arab, as John McMullen once whipped his step-daughter Sarah for staying in Newcastle over night. Now he makes it clear to Sarah that no Protestant is going to accompany her up the aisle.

Like Tom, David is gentle, good and kind, and he is better educated than Sarah, to whom he will indeed be married. His education is a significant reason why she is attracted to him. Their relationship is also built, in Sarah's mind, on her belief that she will find peace with him. She is tirelessly grateful to David for rescuing her from the dire circumstances of her own life. There is no avoiding the conclusion that Tom is David and Catherine is Sarah, and no avoiding Catherine's censure of all that David and Tom represent. The question Catherine is asking is, When David's gentle approach has worked its transformation and removed the need for her gratitude, what then? Will she not tire of David's intellectually superior little world?

Enter John Hetherington, quite his brother David's opposite pole. While David is civilised, educated and morally good, John has a natural, spontaneous streak and a physicality about him which has quite passed David by; he is also up in arms about the exploitation of the Jarrow workers. There is an immediate, magnetic attraction, which so takes Sarah by surprise that she makes a point of avoiding John until, on New Year's Eve (when else?) he bumps into her in the lane as she is leaving the Hetheringtons' house to wish her mother Happy New Year.

Much against her better judgement, Sarah agrees to let John accompany her. It is one of those Tyneside nights, a darkened sky spattered with whispy, ethereal clouds moving fast across a full moon. She remembers

David correcting her when she had described a similar scene by saying that the moon was racing across the sky. He had told her, no, it was the clouds moving, not the moon, which had taken some of the magic out of it. But now, in order to set them against the strong wind, the great hulking figure of John grabs her by the hand and sets off on a run along the river bank, laughing and whooping and pulling her along, seeming actually to be racing the moon. The occasional sound of song and rejoicing vaguely impinges on consciousness as they pass within earshot of groups of people seeing in the New Year, but it is as if John and she are in another dimension, untouched by the world of reality. Finally, exhausted, she manages to pull him up, and she leans against a wall panting heavily and laughing, and calling him a mad fool.

It is significant that Catherine has chosen as context for their coming together her own experience of the spontaneous, intuitional Kate racing the moon. Nothing could recommend the relationship more completely in her grammar of the Mythic North. And there, on the pavement, out it all spills. He holds her by the shoulders, she feels his hot breath upon her face, he speaks to her in a hoarse whisper and tells her the effect she has on him. His body is pressed against hers and she feels every part of him through their clothes. She gasps David's name, but he sweeps it aside and envelops her, his open mouth coming down from a great height upon her ear.

She struggles to free herself, but as his mouth moves round to her face she realises she is submitting to him. There are no secrets left between them. Catherine even has John chide Sarah for finding his brother David's gentle kind of loving enough. It seems so unlikely in the context of the fictional relationship, when John would surely want to have her forget David, that one cannot help suspecting that the author is finding a vicarious pleasure in belittling David, as much as in celebrating the primitive force in John.

Sarah reacts aggressively, but can only recommend her husband for being morally good. John grants her as much, telling Sarah that he doesn't want to hurt David, and then returns to the business of demonstrating his passion. They do not make love that New Year's night, but together, bathed in the moon's pale, haunting light, they discover lands that no conscience ever reaches, so that when they stand apart, holding each other only with their eyes, their breath hanging on the cold night air between them, they might as well have done.

In the symbolic language of the Cookson *oeuvre*, racing the moon identifies the primitive force of John and Sarah's passion with Kate's intuitive spontaneity, which is itself identified in Catherine's mind with her own creative inspiration and the freedom that writing the novels gave her. Here, it comes together with the image of the moon, which has been a symbol of creativity and inspiration since time immemorial.

David and Tom are left out in the cold. They are not authentic, they do not understand what Sarah has found with John, they cannot connect with what Catherine has discovered through Kate and has herself experienced in the privacy of her own composing room.

It is rough, physical, intuitional: anti-education, primitive. There couldn't have been a more complete disposal of Tom, except by the means by which she chose to dispose of David in the novel – she blows him up with a bomb!

The early 1960s was a busy time, not only writing two or more novels a year, but serials for *Women's Realm* and novels under the pen name Catherine Marchant (a name selected by her agent, John Smith, to distinguish her main output from the *Women's Realm* commissioned romances). And *Our Kate* had been in the works since 1956.

In June 1962, six years after beginning her life story to date, she wrote to Mannie, 'Mrs Johnson [her secretary] says she has had a bellyful of biography.'

Catherine sent the latest version to John Smith, but by 1963 she was re-writing it again, and in that year her publisher, Macdonalds, asked her in to discuss writing childrens books.

She was also still giving talks all over the country. 'This side of the business is getting out of bounds,' she wrote to Mannie in November 1964. 'I have now got bookings up to the end of November 1965.' Her publishing schedule was becoming as full of reprints as of new books – in that year both *The Blind Miller* and *Hannah Massey* were reprinting, 'But oh it's tiring! I went to Margate last week [to give a talk] and had to stay overnight, then to Ashford and got held up in this "Go Slow". Tom was waiting on the station for me around 12 pm.'

Of course Tom was waiting at the station. One aspect of Catherine's life increasingly required Tom's attention – illness. She still suffered regular nosebleeds, which no doctor had yet managed to diagnose, but now it was aggravating a bout of neuritis (pain due to inflammation of the nerves). Shortly afterwards there was an exploratory operation in the area of the appendix, which revealed nothing. It was about this time, too, that Catherine developed cramps in her elbow and was advised by Mannie to speak her novels into a tape recorder, the 'Grundig Dictator' which can be seen amongst other effects on permanent exhibition at the South Shields Museum.

Catherine was constantly suffering from ill health, or feared she was, a symptom of the pressures under which she was putting herself and Tom, whose sympathetic tones were being tuned to concert pitch.

Yet, when fit, she was capable of amazing feats of stamina and strength.

Above: the tree, still alive in the garden of Loreto today, against which Catherine would lean and feel the pulsating life force surging, empowering and reaching down to its farthest roots in the dense undersoil.

Left: the swimming pool built in the grounds of Loreto, tangible evidence of Tom's creative efforts to encourage an environment in which she could alleviate her self-imposed stress, lose herself in the rhythms of swimming, and nurture the side of her from which she became separated.

A three-day storm had her sawing fallen trees in the area day-in-day-day out to clear them, and Mannie remarked that when he first visited them, 'Kitty was in the garden at Loreto, working like a man, muscular in her technique, laying steps and pulling out tulips…' Soon she would have her own swimming pool built next to the house, conquer her fear of water and become a daily swimmer.

Then, in 1964, there was a major development, a move by Macdonalds to launch her properly in America. The publishers had done little to sell Catherine even to the British public. Her talks and constant stream of books and media interviews had provided the momentum of her success. Intervention was so unusual that when her editor at *Woman's Realm* on one occasion told her to

'When we arrived,' Mannie recalled, 'Kitty was in the garden at Loreto, working like a man, muscular in her technique, laying steps and pulling out tulips...' But she worked in the garden to Tom's design.

rewrite a piece that she felt was not up to scratch, Catherine was astonished and at first outraged. Then the editor took her through it and explained what was needed, and mutual respect and a greatly enhanced piece of writing ensued. In 1964 Macdonalds did get involved, however. The idea was to create a paperback bestseller in the USA, where Catherine had only been published inter-

'Once back in the North I was homesick not for Hastings or the South of England but for Loreto, that lovely house and garden,' said Catherine.

mittently and in hardcover. They wanted something set in Jarrow, as *The Fifteen Streets* had been, but big, sprawling and farther back in history. There had been a suggestion of setting it in Roman times, but as Catherine and Tom came in from working in the garden one winter's day, Tom put on the kettle and came up with the idea of focusing the story on Palmers Shipyard.

Palmers Shipyard, just a short walk west of the New Buildings, at once triggered Catherine's imagination. She had witnessed as a child the wonderful and terrifying sight of dockers pouring out of Palmers when the buzzers blew, floating like black lava down to the mercantile dock and Jarrow High Street. And was not her childhood vision of Hell sparked by the rose-tinted glow in the sky

Tom had put the kettle on and while they were waiting for it to boil, he came up with the idea of setting a novel around Palmers Shipyard in Jarrow. So, Katie Mulholland *was born.*

Building births at Palmers Yard. Jarrow, in its heyday, 1894. Thanks to the enterprising Charles Mark Palmer employment in shipbuilding in the North East rose from 4,000 men in 1862 to 50,000 by 1911, almost half of the national total.

when the Palmers blast furnaces tipped?

Since the 19th century, the shipyard had been the throbbing heart of Jarrow, the steel heart. Integration of the steel, coal and shipbuilding empires is what had brought it to the fore. Palmer-built and Palmer-owned iron colliers would take coal from mines owned by John Bowes & Partners (of which Charles Mark Palmer was a director) to London, calling at Port Mulgrave on the way back to ship a load of iron ore for the Palmer furnaces. Setting a story around this was an exciting prospect indeed, and how appropriate that her breakthrough novel should be attached to such drive and enthusiasm. For Palmer had turned Jarrow, a village, into a town for mining gold out of steel.

Tom again had been the key – this time to Catherine's first 19th-century historical, a genre that would produce novels such as *The Glass Virgin, The Dwelling Place, Feathers in the Fire,* the *Mallen* trilogy, *The Girl, The Cinder Path* and the *Tilly Trotter* trilogy, and lead Catherine back, ever closer to the industrial source of Kate's world, giving new depth to the mythology.

This was a very important turning point. *Katie Mulholland* came out in 1967, and it took her back into her grandma Rose's time, to the roots of the industrial revolution. Palmers had been at the epicentre. The company's launching of the iron-hulled John Bowes, the first collier really to make money, revolutionised the shipping of coal, but it also revolutionised the shipbuilding industry. Suddenly shipyards were crowding the banks of the Tyne and by the turn of the century, Tyneside shipbuilders were responsible for a quarter of the world's tonnage. The shipbuilding Palmers and the coal-mining Bowes linked up in a massively successful partnership, and this cross-industry strategy was repeated across the industrial board, whether companies were originally in coal, ships, railways, glass or chemicals, partnership became the way forward. When, a century later, Catherine began her research she found the company helpful, but still reeling from the time they helped an author in the 1930s. Sir Charles Mark Palmer's grandson promised her all the help possible, but hoped she wouldn't sell them down the line as the family felt Ellen Wilkinson had in her book, *A Town That Was Murdered.*

It was Wilkinson who famously led the 200 unemployed workers to march from Jarrow to London in 1936. She presented a petition to parliament calling for government action on their behalf, and three years later concluded in her book: 'On their skill and their toil has been built England's industrial revolution. They were crowded into hovels, their children starved and died, and on their sacrifice great capital has been accumulated.' Protestations by Reny and others that Catherine exaggerated conditions in which she grew up seem rather unfairly placed in the light of that level of rhetoric.

Catherine felt, after the unusual amount of research for her book, that she could speak for the working man, and probably make pig iron. The political message is characterised by her personal experience as much as by the research, however, and is welcome for it. She blames the unions for making their revolution a battleground between 'us and us' (inter-union conflict) as much as between 'them and us' (employer-worker conflict), and for all sides failing to galvanise the concept of worker/company participation. But that is

Right: Palmers Boiler Shop. Before Katie Mulholland, *Catherine hadn't been published in paperback in the American market. Now they had asked for a 'big read' and she had obliged with many hundreds of thousands of words. She had researched the Palmer family and Palmers Shipyard. She had gone into Ellen Wilkinson's politics; and in the end she felt she could speak for the working man, and probably make pig iron. But now the Americans wanted her to cut the length of the manuscript by a third. She bit her lip and with grim determination set about the soul-destroying job of cutting. Her advisers told her that this could be a very big break, and many still feel it was then she was properly discovered.*

not what the book is about. In *Katie Mulholland*, the author invests the heroine with her own energy and gumption, her own against-all-odds spirit. The theme is of endurance rewarded. And with it the author's rewards were suitably enhanced, too.

The other great development of Catherine's novels occurred in the early 1970s – from *The Dwelling Place* and *Feathers In The Fire* on. It came from the charge they received from the Durham and Northumberland countryside. The best loved novels of the 1970s and 1980s are set in and beyond a rectangle of landscape more or less demarcated by Haltwhistle (in the north west), Alston (in the south west), Haydon Bridge (in the north east), and Allenheads (in the south east), and they attest to an increasing number of trips up into the Allendale region that Catherine was making.

The Mallen Streak takes a charge not only from the author's illegitimacy, but from Shap Fell and Alston Moor, the staggeringly beautiful drive from Penrith, on which Catherine first became afraid of wilderness landscape. 'I had the most strange feeling, touching of terror,' she told me. The road took her over Hartside Top, almost 2,000 feet above sea level, and there are many opportunities for terror, and possibilities too for the site of 'the great fall', where

The Northumberland moors between Alston and Allendale Town provide many settings for Catherine's novels in this period, such as Feathers In The Fire *(between Plenmeller Common and Whitfield),* The Girl *(the edge of Acton Moor),* The Tinker's Girl *(over Whitfield Moor) and the* Mallen *trilogy, which was sourced in one of many trips made to the area from Hastings. This was special in that they drove from Hastings in the south east to Penrith, north and west, and thence over Shap Fell and Alston moors, a huge undertaking across some of the most stunning wilderness landscape in England.*

The route over Shap Fell and Alston Moor. 'He stopped the car and I got out and sat on the footboard. There was nothing surrounding us for miles except about 20 yards from the road there stood the wreck of an old house. I understood that it had once been an inn where the men driving horses over Shap Fell stopped and rested and had a drink. But now it only showed a broken roof, a door hanging on its hinges.'

Thomas Mallen's illegitimate son, Donald, a dark, brooding character given to long silences and bursts of temper, is killed by his consumptive half-brother, Matthew.

There is more than one possible site, too, for the 'wreck of an old house', which becomes a place of refuge for Matthew and Constance Mallen in another significant moment in the novel, and which Catherine told me she had espied when Tom brought the car to a halt over Alston moor:

He stopped the car and I got out and sat on the footboard. There was nothing surrounding us for miles except about 20 yards from the road there stood the wreck of an old house. I understood, after, it had once been an inn where the men driving horses over Shap Fell stopped and rested and had a drink. But now it only showed a broken roof, a door hanging on its hinges. The walls were standing, but the window frames and every piece of wood seemed to have been stripped from it. I stared at it and the sight of it fell into my subconscious and lay there working until I thought up the story of *The Mallen Streak* and this dirty filthy wreck of a house became the

setting for the conception of a child by two of the main characters in the book. There are many characters in the book, but these two were important and it is where they were trying to shelter from a terrible storm together with their horses and expressed their love for each other (which was a dangerous thing, as the girl was engaged to her lover's half-brother). I described the house, the filthy condition and their coming together, all as if I had thought it up on the day of terror on the fells of Northumberland.

It was a significant day because it was the first time Tom had driven Catherine over these moors on their way north. Before this they had always gone by train and made forays out. This was a major trip which will have taken many hours from Hastings and it had a significant effect both on Catherine and Tom, and on the later period of novels, which dig deep into the emotional contours of the landscape of the area. Their explorations took Catherine deeper into the history of her people, into the living culture of the lead-mining industry (in *The Girl* and *A Dinner of Herbs*), out of which native Northumbrians arose long before the industrial revolution drew them down into the towns of the Tyne.

Contact with the Allendale lead mining industry (see the snow-clad Killhope Mine, above) took Catherine farther back in time than her grandma Rose had been able to remember for the settings of her novels, closer to the roots of her people's culture, to the element that 'comes from far back and threads the people of this area'. Novels like The Girl *and* A Dinner of Herbs *were the result.*

158

'This countryside is raw, and it is with me and I feel it. You cannot alter the seasons, and up here the seasons are rougher than those in the South and I imbibe them…and there is *a harshness.'*

It is hardly surprising that Catherine found this landscape so beguiling. It threw back at her the raw essence of herself that she had uncovered in her breakdown, and which was influencing her relationship with Tom and was increasingly to find expression in the novels. In our first interview on August 7, 1985, having myself just driven through Allendale, where she was then living, I marvelled at the beauty. She sat me down and said, 'Up here I *know* that I am in my own country, not soft like the downs, nor flat like the fens (that Tom likes so much). This countryside is *raw*, and it is with me and I feel it. You cannot alter the seasons, and up here the seasons are rougher than those in the South and I imbibe them…and there *is* a harshness.'

At just about the time she was embarking on *Katie Mulholland*, Rosemary Barker, Aunt Sarah's niece, first met Catherine and Tom. Rosemary had married an accountant, son of a miner from the South East

159

Durham coalfields, by name of Foster Barker. Today they live in Loreto, but had lived in Scotland until 1964 when Foster's firm posted him to London and they bought a house at Iver Heath in Buckinghamshire.

'Aunt Sarah came down to visit us,' Foster recalled. 'She had always kept in touch with Kitty, and as Buckinghamshire was closer to Hastings than Birtley, she suggested we come down and meet her. I was totally overawed with her really. I was about 28 and quite impressionable and hadn't been to big houses. I had just come from the North of England. She liked us immediately and told us to come again. Then we brought our children down and she loved them. She would hug the kids, wait for them coming down the drive, but she didn't like children in the house, messing about on her furniture.

'We once spent a week here and were very honoured to be invited to stay with our children. She told us this, she was very straight: "Yours are the only children ever allowed in my house." Children never got beyond the kitchen, where the Aga was, unless they wanted to go to the toilet. She allowed ours to come into this room, the drawing room, but no other children had been allowed in here. But they did like our children and they were well behaved, I suppose."

I marvelled at the contrast with the early days at the Hurst, where children

The Tyne sweeping north of Hexham. 'Up here I know that I am in my own country, not soft like the downs, nor flat like the fens (that Tom likes so much).' But Catherine did not attach herself to this majestic area for long, preferring the harder country of the Northumberland moors.

were always welcome, and asked Rosemary how theirs had enjoyed a week's holiday walking on egg shells.

'We didn't disturb her day. We went down on the beach with the children. We had the children out all day. We'd bring them in late afternoon, bath them, they would come in here (to the drawing room) and have a little chat with Auntie Kitty and Uncle Tom. Then they would be put to bed and we would have our meal and play bridge, so the evening was spent with them. Kitty and Tom loved playing bridge.'

It was a far cry from the days when Tom brought his pupils home, when he and Catherine messed about on boats, when Tom had been laying the ground rules for a bit of family fun. They didn't go on holiday anymore and Tom had left the school Scout Troop in 1963, the year he became Senior Maths Master. But the real difference was his own status at home. The Barkers told me, and Cousin Sarah remembered this, too, that if Tom went off in the garden, after just a few minutes you would hear Catherine's voice, full of pathos on the breeze, 'Tom… Tom…' And Tom would come. He never complained. Other people had also begun to notice Catherine's increasing control of him and his ready submission to her will.

She looked at the cold harsh landscape and it threw back at her something of her own self, something of that side of her that civilised society would have her dispel. It was a side that began to tell in her books and one with which, in the real light of day, her husband, Tom, increasingly had to contend.

'I remember one occasion,' Mannie told me, 'late at night after dinner, she ordered Tom, "Go and do the dishes," and Tom obediently made his way to the kitchen, but my wife Rita stood his ground for him, saying, "No, go to bed. We will do the dishes." I think Rita and I did the dishes in the end.' This was no isolated incident, it became characteristic of Catherine's behaviour. She had also begun to belittle him in public. Whatever he did – gardening, baking cakes, playing piano – she could do it better. It was almost embarrassing for those around, though Catherine didn't seem to notice.

When a journalist took Tom up on it, he said, 'People always assume I'm in the background and always was throughout our marriage. But I never believed I was inferior, deep inside myself. With her beside me there was nothing I felt I could not do. There was this person who to me exuded such magnetism that deep down I must have been craving. She believes in herself and by golly, she made me believe in her and me too… I can't bear to be apart from her even for a little while.'

People talk of the novels as therapy, but writing them didn't change Catherine, rather they exercised elements of her damaged nature – often to electrifying effect, as I will show. This may well have been palliative, but effected no cure, as Catherine herself averred when we first met. She was 79 and could say, 'Fear has been the single most important emotion of my childhood, of my whole life, and it *still* is, right up to this very moment.' With the fear resided her aggression and the need to control. The novels did nothing to change that. They didn't so much drain it out of her as provide a safe channel for it.

The reason they were merely palliative is that they were a regression. They returned her to her place of suffering and allowed her to belong in it, which actually put an end to the existential striving that had taken her away from the North and might have allowed her to develop beyond her trauma. Had the break from her past in 1929 proved clean, had Kate not come down to live in Hastings in 1932, had she and Tom been blessed with a family of their own, then the prognosis might have been different, and she may never have written the novels, or at least these novels.

It is to Catherine's eternal credit that she attempted the progressive solution. As psychoanalyst Erich Fromm wrote, 'Each individual is confronted with the same alternative; his margin of freedom not to choose the regressive solution [to the existential split from family, or 'mother' culture] in a society

When Catherine became successful, Tom slipped wholly under her iron-willed control, and 'control' for the first time became a feature of the novels, often in scenes of sado-masochism. In 1969 Tom was retired early so that he could be at her beck and call twenty-four hours a day. In 1971 she moved out of the small room where Kate had died and installed a huge desk in the lounge upstairs, with a little seat for him to sit at a typewriter on the end of it. The novels gave her a forum for the complete exercise of her will. She wanted her hand alone on the tiller and all hands on deck, her publishers included. Tom said he wanted it no other way, but the stress had already begun to tell.

that has chosen it is indeed small – yet it exists. But great effort, clear thinking, and guidance by the humanists is necessary.'

Breaking free in 1929 was absolutely the right instinct. She got out and moved forward, but Kate caught up with her before she managed to make the separation complete. Then came the breakdown and the novels, which brought her back to the start, to the place she had resisted and from which she had tried to escape. As Doris Johnson astutely pointed out, 'She ended up still chained to Tyneside.'

But was it a regression in the sense of failure? The strategy of returning to the fold in which her childhood trauma occurred arose not out of escapism but from the heavy dose of reality thinking that her nervous breakdown had administered. Also, the humanist solution would never have satisfied Catherine. The lovelessness of her childhood was always attached to a need for love, and even at her most controlling there was the capacity for it and the remembrance of that 'divine vision' of love in its first unfolding beneath the Tyne Dock arches, which she associated with God.

Nevertheless, while imaging her trauma in the illegitimacy and crippled-ness of her characters had worked commercially, from an emotional point of view it had been less successful. She and Tom found there was a price to pay. At first, in the creative state of writing the novels, she enjoyed a kind of equi-librium in the womb of her people, but the bitterness and hate remained and the

Her control of Tom, her belittling of him in public, her constant need of him, did not mean that she did not love him. She did, and he knew that she loved him, but it was not the love of the Mary Ann Shaughnessy years.

The novels, their content and their success, had confined her in a shell of self-absorption in which her childhood trauma was getting the complete attention it had always craved. Her relationship with the outside world, her hus-band included, was now cast in terms of that.

There was sacrifice, and self-sacrifice was in Tom's nature. You might say that they met their destiny in each other, but people who knew them at this time talk of a real sadness in him.

The old Grammar School (above) close to Queen's Road in Hastings, where a pupil caught Tom in a state of deep depression.

'I just felt desperately sad for him. He had such skills, such talent and clearly a devotion to her. And yet it [their relationship] was so destructive. And she was destructive of herself and of people around her.'

emotions she exercised in this state were increasingly no more paradisaical than they had been in reality, for there was no ultimate relief. At the same time she became tied to the palliative and dare not stop – 'I can't stop now. The doctors ask me to stop. Tom begs me to stop. But I can't stop,' she said in desperation in 1969. That was the nature of the beggar's ride to hell.

Tom became wholly involved in the process and bore the brunt of her obsessive preoccupation. Her control over him was brought to the level of a benevolent sort of sadism, benevolent because, as Tom said, he wanted it no other way, though the pressure was beginning to tell. He first began suffering the migraines in 1961. In that year Catherine told Mannie of 'an apparatus attached to the beams in the attic by which he [Tom] stretches the neck.' By 1964 he had an appointment with a specialist, and Catherine wrote that the specialist said to him: 'The trouble is you're a perfectionist.' The specialist realised at once that the migraines were down to stress.

While I was writing this book I received a call from an ex-pupil of Tom's called Steve Blower, who gave me an extraordinary window onto Tom at this time. Steve had attended the Grammar School in the 1960s, he telephoned after watching a television documentary about Catherine and Tom.

I was there from 1961 to 1967. Tom was my teacher in the A stream. He was very small, a very tiny guy, but he had a presence about him that was quite compelling. There was something very gentle...and yet he had the ability to command the attention and respect of a group of thirty adolescents. We had another connection, Mrs Stanbridge, who lived next door to us, was actually Mrs Cookson's cleaner. She was given a signed copy of every one of her books as they were published.

One thing I remember... I was watching a TV documentary about them and I was really powerfully reminded of something that I want to share with you. I was in my last year... perhaps it was the summer term 1966. I had done my exams and I was just hanging around waiting for the results before I left. I was walking back along Queen's Road in Hastings and found Tom Cookson standing on the pavement almost as though he was in another world. He was completely not with it, totally distracted, focused on something that was not the world around him. I remember standing next to him for what seemed a long time and gradually his attention came back, as it were, to the present. And I just said to him, 'Are you OK, sir?' And he said, 'Hah, umm...' And I felt I had to say *something*, and so I said, 'My Mum loves your wife's books.' And he said, 'Oh... Good.' And that was it!

I knew that the Queen's Road was near the original site of the Grammar School, and that by 1966 the school had moved to another site far away. I asked Steve what he thought Tom was doing there. He said: 'I would walk that way back to my friend's house and then walk along to the centre of the town and catch the bus home. I don't know what he was doing there. It was almost like he had been deposited there by some force. It certainly wasn't... we were no longer at the school site nearby. Possibly he had been drawn back there... he was certainly distracted, in a personal reverie.'

'But he wasn't happy?'

'Absolutely not. There was a real sadness about him, and when I was watching that programme it sort of clicked into place for me really. I just felt *desperately* sad for him. He had such skills, such talent and clearly a devotion to her. And yet it was so destructive. And she was destructive of herself and of people around her... Ultimately he was a free man, he had choices and that was the choice he made, not an easy one by any means.'

1969 was an eventful year, one in which Catherine got a great deal of what she wanted, most of all that Tom retire and become 'her complete factotum,' as Tony Weeks-Pearson had described him. It was also the year they met Dr Gabb, the Hastings doctor who arranged for a new treatment for Tom's migraines to be sent from America and for Catherine to see a specialist in Wimpole Street, near Harley Street in London, an appointment that resulted in skin grafts for her bleeding and the diagnosis of an inherited blood disorder called telangiectasis. Catherine, thrilled at last to know why she had been bleeding since 1924, would become something of a research guinea pig, and later donated millions for research into the disease.

By this time Rosemary and Foster Barker had moved to Upminster on the east side of London, making the journey to Loreto easier, and they were visiting Catherine and Tom regularly. While house hunting, Foster had taken digs and met a woman called Jane Bennett, who had an interest in antiques. 'We would buy a *Hendon Times* on a Thursday night and go around these houses, mainly Jewish people around Golders Green, and Jane would be buying the furniture. I told Kitty about it, and she said, "Oh, if you get anything get it for me," and that is how it all started.'

Just at the time she was beginning to make serious money, Catherine had been presented with something to spend it on, something which fitted perfectly her life-long picture (first seen when pressing herself against the slime-dripping walls of the Tyne Dock arches) of the splendour in which she planned to live. She had been interested in good furniture since the early '30s, when she would put money down on a piece week-by-week.

'I'd ring Kitty up, reversing the charges from London, always on a Thursday evening,' said Foster, 'and if I didn't ring her, by the time I got back from London to Essex – I would be in the house for half an hour – and she would be on the telephone: "You haven't rung. Have you been out? Have you bought anything?" Maybe I'd say, "I've seen a nice table, a nice three-piece suite, curtains..." – always about £5, £10.'

Catherine had not lost her taste for a bargain, indeed the beauty of the antiques was one thing and the bargain element was about as important. 'She saw me as an opportunity to go out and buy nice things *cheap*. She

Feathers In The Fire *country, the novel in which Catherine openly examined her psychic crippledness and justified her bitterness and resentment in a scream against Nature on the part of humanity, casting herself in the role of Amos, the illegitimate, born with two fleshy protrusions where his legs should have been.*

always liked a bargain. Very canny woman. I don't think she ever bought a new thing in her life. I mean, that chandelier and a matching one there.' Foster pointed to the lights in the drawing room of Loreto, where we were sitting. 'That was £10, and those wall lights were £5. Every room in this house… I bought all the curtains for her (which she paid for), beautiful, magnificent, down to the floor. She came to London for the three-piece suite that was in here. I called her, said I'd seen it. She said, "Buy it!" I said, "No, it's £100, come and see it."

'So, when she was speaking up in London we went to Hendon. She wasn't so well known then, she was only known in the libraries, and I remember we went into this house, it was a doctor's wife, and she thought she was the real lady and all the rest of it and really put Kitty down, and there was real venom when Catherine didn't get the suite! The woman already had it in mind for someone else, who she thought was of a better standing than Kitty to sell it to. When we got out I said, "She wasn't very nice, was she Kitty?" Kitty said, "Don't worry Foster, she'll be in one of my books."

'A lot of the stuff she had up North we also bought. Do you remember that lovely sofa table, the pink French suite? We bought that. And then clothes.

We bought her clothes out of Oxfam. Do you remember that green dress with the gold thread through, she wore it to do lots of interviews? I bought that for her…from Oxfam. Up in Hampstead.

'Then, in 1969 she asked us to look after the house while they went to Jersey, to look to buy a house there.' Catherine's success was taking her into the Supertax bracket and the law at that time allowed her only 19p in the pound, so she was advised to become a tax exile. The very idea showed a hopeless misunderstanding as to what Catherine was about. The trip was a disaster and included an upset with a drunken passenger on the flight home. Catherine was not short of reasons to block the move, but the decider, recalled Foster, was that the house chosen for them turned out to be next to a prison.

'We expected them to stay a week, but in two or three days they were back,' Rosemary added. 'They said, "No, no don't go home," so we stayed here the rest of the time, and that is when we read, in manuscript form, *Feathers In The Fire*. She left it for us to read, and asked us what we thought. It was one of her good books.'

It certainly was, if 'good' can allow weird. Amos, the central character, was inspired by Jackie Halliday, the East Jarrow coalman who lived in Bogey Hill, half a mile to the west of the New Buildings. 'Jackie Halliday used to sell coal, tuppence a bucket,' Catherine told me when we first met, 'and as a child I thought his legs were buried in the coal. I didn't work it out that I should have seen them sticking through the cart. I very rarely went up Bogey Hill, but one day I saw this "thing" going across the back lane and I recognised his face and for the first time I realised that the man had no legs and I stopped and stared at him. Well, you know, a child's horror can affect someone, and I saw it in that man's face. It was misty; the face had gone, but the feeling remained, and I felt that I had to portray that in some way.'

As in the case of *Fanny McBride*, the image stayed with her and she brought it back to self, identifying completely with her main character. Catherine's illegitimate status is shared by Amos, who is the child of Master Farmer Angus McBain and servant girl, Molly Geare, and Catherine knows Amos's anger and hurt, which is the aggression and hate of her own childhood.

Amos is an outcast, a victim of selfish passion, a cripple and gives rise to disgust. This disgust is significant. Grace Rouse, as she approached breakdown in *The Garment*, felt disgust with herself, unclean inside. This feeling was with Catherine from the moment she got it into her head that illegitimacy was not just a term of abuse, but a station lower than the rest of humanity that applied to her, so low that she had assumed she did not merit a birth certificate.

She had been asked for one by Matron Silverlock when she registered at the workhouse and, assuming there wasn't one, had spilled her shame out, when in fact Kate had had one all the time, it even carried the name of her father, Alexander Davies. Catherine's problem flowed from her mistaken conviction that she had been alienated all her life on account of being irredeemably 'base-born', being born lower than the lowest, when in fact her alienation stemmed from the hate and bitter resentment she expressed over the dissemblance

Feathers In The Fire is set on Whitfield Moor. Above: the Tor where the cripple Amos appears with his half-sister, Jane. There is pain, violence, rape and an overt instance of sado-masochism in it. Prevalent throughout is a sense of self-disgust and hate.

of her birth, from which she cannot shake herself free. Self-disgust and resentment permeate *Feathers In The Fire*. Plagued by Nature and disowned by his father, the response of the 'legless thing' is bitter resentment, which leads to savage retribution in the novel. Amos sets about murdering his father, Angus McBain, and repays the sisterly love, innocent of pity and richly authentic, of McBain's legitimate daughter, Jane, with attempted rape and the murder of her betrothed.

The novel offers a clear window into how hating oneself can twist feelings in the most aberrant fashion, and the conviction with which the narrative is delivered refutes any criticism of self-indulgence, sensationalism or extravagance, and yet there seems to be more to this novel than Catherine examining her misplaced resentment at her own illegitimacy. There is pain, violence, rape and overt sado-masochism – the essence of all of which is *control*.

From the publication of *Feathers In The Fire* on, a number of novels explore this theme of aberrant control in terrifying close focus and reveal a strange preoccupation on the part of the author with her newfound ability to exercise control over her life and Tom. This, of course, is what Mrs Thornton feared would happen if Maggie Rowan was given rein, the idea that once

Maggie felt power she would be like the beggar on horseback and ride to hell.

Catherine's final plea to me was to make people feel the scar that Kate had left upon her. Kate's personal guilt has been wildly exaggerated, but the scar was there nonetheless – left by the withdrawal of her mother's love at birth and the compounding of this six years later, following the chimney-piece episode, when her surrogate parents were also let go. The aberrant nature of these novels – *Feathers In The Fire*, *The Whip*, *The Cinder Path*, *A Dinner of Herbs*, and others besides – testifies to the scar far better than autobiography because we know there is something here that was not present in the early 'social histories', something that tells us that despite all the work Tom put in and the effect upon her of writing the novels, all is not yet quite right.

In *Feathers In The Fire*, after it is discovered that Molly is pregnant, Angus McBain, who has taken her and is the father of her child, subjects her to a public horse-whipping. The reason he does this is, so he suggests, that people will expect him to get out of Molly the name of the father of her unborn child and bring him to book. But, of course, both Molly and McBain know that McBain himself is the father. Yet Molly does not resist his plan, nor does she name him as the father of her child – doing so would certainly have prevented

The splinter of ice in her heart, cut from the cold North, fashioned some of her very best fiction.

the whipping, which goes forward as a piece of sado-masochism with overt sexual connotation. Innocent Jane McBain rumbles exactly what is going on and takes Molly up on it afterwards, getting into a real state, unable to cope with the feelings that her knowledge has raised in her mind. All she can do is beat her little fists on Molly, while Molly wards off the blows and, clearly embarrassed at what Jane suspects, pleads with her to keep quiet about it. Jane knows that Molly and her father are lovers, that's one thing, but what she cannot come to terms with is that Molly let McBain whip her, seeming to participate freely in her own humiliation, the two of them revelling in his domination over her.

Later, McBain and Molly's sin is made manifest in Amos's deformity, and is nearly compounded in the drowning of their child after he is born with a head, two arms, but no legs, just short stumps and fleshy flippers for feet. Catherine was feeling what Jackie Halliday must have felt when, as a young man, he found that he had no legs, and we can begin to appreciate the strength of feeling associated with her own 'deformity'. Again there is a deeply moral, 'David' character to remind us how different Catherine's psychology might have been.

This dire frame of mind pursued Catherine into the next novel, *Pure as The Lily*, published in 1972, where Mary Walton disfigures Lally's lover and burns her alive. So terrible is the sadistic disposal of Lally, who is a symbol of creativity in the novel, that Mary suffers a stroke, and her daughter, Betty, turns in a scene of terrible retribution, taunting her paralysed mother with what she has done and then leaving her to stew in bed, her arms lying limp beside her, eyelids flickering, saliva dripping from the corner of her mouth, strange guttural sounds filling the room. Daughter damns mother with the hope that she will suffer life in this way for years and years. Then Betty turns and walks out, and we feel that the scar that Mary has left upon her is a good deal less visible.

Sadism is a theme in the novels for the next ten years or more. One thinks, in particular, of *The Cinder Path* (1978), *The Whip* (1983) and *A Dinner of Herbs* (1985). The cinder path is a place of violent abuse by a father upon his sons across generations. Early on, Charlie McFell was told he was a loser, that he was born a loser. His father, Edward, is a warped personality,

damage done by his own father, William, who, in 1858, had bought the farm, where first Edward and then Charlie and his sister, Betty, were brought up. When Edward was just 8, his father threw him down onto the rough surface of a cinder path and beat him with a birch. The pain and humiliation to which his father regularly subjected him (and any young miscreant on the farm) is made doubly wounding by the knowledge that his father has laid the path expressly for that purpose.

This strangely symbolic, black strip of sharp cinders, led otherwise uselessly from the farm to the stream which gave Moor Burn Farm its name. The dead-end cinder track was never trod; no-one could possibly want to use it as a track. It led nowhere, other than into the dark, obsessional reaches of its creator's mind, and on into the mind of the son, Edward, too.

Again, there is this feeling of something weird going on, the idea is itself so strange. Not only is there sadism, but again, as in *Feathers*, there is sexual connotation. When farm hand Ginger Slater's 'narrow buttocks' get the treatment, Polly Benton watches, one hand to her mouth in shock horror, but the other gathering her skirts up to expose not only her boots, but the bare flesh of her shins. In the context of the times this is suggestive indeed.

Again, in *The Whip*, Emma Molinero, who is part of a travelling show and skilled with knives and whips, has her implements turned on her in a pages-long build-up to the most terrible, violent denouement, with, once again, sexual innuendo – her nightdress is, with a savage tug, ripped clean down to the hem by psychopath Luke Yorkless. Cracking the whip, Luke swings round and brings Emma's whip flashing across her face. Her body bounces on the floor, her screams deafen her, blood pours out of her and he rolls her over and over again with his instrument of torture. There is no part of her body which the whip does not reach, and when he is tired he stands there gasping, and assures her that he has only just begun.

In *A Dinner of Herbs* Kate Makepeace comes clean, pointing out that the female in every species is more deadly and bloodthirsty than the male. I asked Rosemary Barker whether that was true of Catherine's family. She laughed and admitted a strength of character among the women, but no genetic answer as to where Catherine's menacing streak came from.

'Sarah, my grandmother was a very formidable woman,' said Rosemary. 'There is nothing weak about any of the women in the family quite frankly. Sarah was the *maitre d'*, she would sit there in her rocking chair and rule the roost, it was as simple as that. And everybody quivered and quaked, loved her to death but nobody would question what she said. That was it, it was law.' So it was a bit of a matriarchal culture into which Catherine had been born? 'Maybe it was because Sarah had such a bad time with the stepfather – there was no way any man would treat her that way again. And Kate as well. They were very strong women, very strong, tough, nice natured, but not vicious or horrible or nasty.'

Doris Johnson comments that 'Catherine had, as many writers do, that splinter of ice in her hear.' What I notice, as the novels move on in this increasingly violent vein through the years, is that the 'excuse' of illegitimacy often takes a back seat, but the author's psychological scars remain very much to the fore.

The later Freud postulates two basic human instincts, the instinct to love and the instinct to destroy – the conditions of existence that these two instincts meet will determine the character of a person. The conditions of existence that Catherine's basic natural instincts met – separated from her mother at birth – were not likely to encourage the instinct to love.

A Dinner of Herbs *is set in the Northumbrian lead-mining district, which Catherine knew so well after she came to live in it.*

Once again, hate is part of the landscape of her fictional characters' lives and reaches its apotheosis in Mary Bannaman, who strings up Hal from a beam high up in a barn, and leaves him to die.

The few photographs that survive of the indigenous people of novels like The Tinker's Girl *and* A Dinner of Herbs *reflect the starkly realistic images conjured up by the author.*

Freud characterised the instinct to love as the life instinct (Eros) and the instinct to destroy as the death instinct (Thanaton). The former impels ever greater unities, the latter divides and conquers and destroys.

In discussing Freud's death instinct, the psychoanalyst Erich Fromm made a distinction between aggression aimed at protecting oneself, the survival instinct, which is benign and common to all animals, and the malignantly destructive version, which has nothing to so with survival and whose aberrant roots are found only in damaged psyches of the human species.

It is that malignant strain of the death instinct with which we are dealing in *A Dinner of Herbs*. Hate never goes away in this novel. It is part of the landscape of the characters' lives and reaches its apotheosis in Mary Bannaman, who strings up Hal like a chicken, from a beam high up in the barn, and leaves him to die. An essential element of the chill in this example of sadistic torture is that a woman is doing it to a man, while the woman's brother looks on, increasingly concerned at what he finds the female of the species capable.

The contraption confining poor Hal in the most unbelievable pain sounds alarmingly like the apparatus attached to the beams in the attic of Loreto by which Tom's neck was stretched, ostensibly to ease his migraines, but there is a serious point in this in that the aberrance and sadism of the novels during this middle to late period were but an imaginative step further along a continuum

on which Catherine's intermittent bouts of aggression and need to control Tom lay. She once assured me she was quite capable of doing anything she gave her characters to do, and allowed me that in *The Girl From Leam Lane*.

Her compulsion to control (and everyone who worked with her felt the sting of it) confirmed the novels as a regressive not a progressive solution – they did not, as she readily admitted, reward her with a cure, and in Freud's terms, her Thanaton remained to the fore during this middle period.

None of this meant that she did not love Tom. She did, and he knew that she loved him, but it was not the love of the Mary Ann Shaughnessy years, nor yet that of the final years. There was sacrifice, but self-sacrifice was in his nature. You might say that Tom was the key that fitted Catherine's lock, that they met their destiny in each other, but both *might* have lived other lives.

In the novel, Hal survives. The love of his life, Mary Ellen gives his dog, Boyo, the job of finding him, and he does so, deep in the barn. Somehow, Mary Ellen and a doctor revive him. Tom Cookson also survived and could still rise up when the occasion arose, as it did in the mid-1970s when Nan Smyth

The real-life counterparts of families like the Bannamans (A Dinner of Herbs) *and the Shalemans* (The Tinker's Tale). *Hate and bitterness passed down through generations in such a closed-in culture, sealed off from the wider world.*

steered him to a sheaf of letters which suggested that his wife had made a mug of him. Foster Barker remembers this period as a succession of bitter moments: 'We were living in Upminster then and we brought Rosemary's father [the miner, Jimmy Tiplady, who helped Catherine research *Maggie Rowan* and is mentioned in the novel's Dedication] to Loreto with Rosemary's mother to see Kitty for the day. We saw Nan Smyth that day, too, and two days later Jimmy had a heart attack, a massive one, and died. I think Rosemary's mother always thought that had we not come down here he would have lived on.' Rosemary agreed: 'My mother hated Loreto. When we bought it from Kitty she just hated it because it had this association with my dad...'

Nan's death followed swiftly when Catherine went away for a few days. Tom had dropped in to see her in the seedy seafront basement to which she had been reduced. Nan told him that after she died he was to go to a drawer where he would find a bundle of letters that she wanted him to have. When Catherine phoned Tom, he didn't mention the letters, but when she told him that she was coming home, he surprised her by saying, in no uncertain terms, that she was to stay where she was until the funeral was over. Catherine asked why and Tom repeated that she should do as he told her.

When, finally, Catherine walked in the front door of Loreto, saying how guilty she felt about missing the funeral, Tom told her to shut up and thrust one of the letters under her nose. Years later, in a taped interview with her first literary agent, John Smith, Catherine said that one of the first letters she read 'went on about all these men that I'd had'. There is then no mention as to how damning the revelations were or how true or false they were. Catherine's interest is only in Nan's hostility towards her, and she reacts as if something has burst in her head. Burned up with hate, she wants to get Nan out of her grave and choke her skeleton.

John is clearly shocked at what he has heard and later shakes his head and talks only of 'a kind of bitterness, absolute bitterness.'

Sarah Lavelle, who, after Catherine and Tom returned to the North in 1976, would work for her cousin, typing her manuscripts, realised long ago that the raw elements in Catherine's fiction were rooted in her own psyche and not mere fancy: 'It was *in* Kitty...

There was a lot of hate, and she didn't have a lot of love, only with Tom. But even Tom nearly left once. I was upstairs in the office in Bristol Lodge (their house in Langley, Northumberland, from 1981) and Kitty was downstairs in the bedroom with Tom. I heard this rumbling going on, but you couldn't make out what was happening between them. And when I went down she said, "Did you hear what was going on?" I said, "No," and she said, "He's got his case out, you know." I said, "His case, whatever for?" She said, "He wants a divorce."

'He had a real up-and-downer with her. Whatever it was about I don't know, but whatever happened between them in their life, Tom was always the one who had to say sorry. He always had to go and kneel by her bed... She twisted things round not just with him but with anybody. I think she didn't like people to be too happy. She seemed to resent if people were happy, too content.'

If she resented people being too happy it was because she knew that Nature was not happy, and hers in particular was sad. In her portrayal of Amos in *Feathers In The Fire* she justified her hate as a kind of psychic scream for all humanity, empathising with him: 'Just imagine, in a tough area like the Tyne, where they are all he-men,' she said to me. 'Is there anything fair in Nature? Ask yourself, Piers, unfairness in Nature, when a mountain can come down and bury people in its mud. Is there anything fair? When a volcano can burst and burn people to death? Is there anything fair in Nature?'

I think that we have seen that Catherine was not made to be happy, she saw too far into things to settle for happiness. Many times she said she envied Sarah's peace of mind, but was clear that her own purpose lay elsewhere. For years Catherine corresponded with an American nun, and there are no prizes for guessing her name – Sister Catherine belongs to the Dominican Sisters of Mission San José in California. In a letter to Tom, written after our Catherine died in 1998, she spells out what she thought her namesake's purpose was:

She honoured me with such attention and trust, and believed in what she saw as goodness in me. Yet it was I who drank from her. She was willing to share her brokenness with the world and as a

'She was willing to share her brokenness with the world and as a result became a giant, cosmic fountain from which all others could drink' Sister Catherine of the Dominican Sisters of Mission San José in California.

result became a giant, cosmic fountain from which all others could drink. Eucharist cannot be shared and eaten unless it is first broken and blessed. Catherine through the ministry of her writing, nourished and strengthened hundreds of thousands of people and gave them courage and purpose just by announcing who she was.

This is, in actuality, the only purpose for our existence. If we do not connect with others and affirm them in their struggles, we miss the whole point. Catherine was so beyond institutions, religions and social affiliations, the confinement of rule and regulation – all that the Kingdom calls us to become.

Catherine made a difference, and not only to those charities that benefited from the many millions of pounds she and Tom donated. She received thousands of letters each year. Here's one picked more or less at random – Mrs Christine Johnson, writing on 27.11.1995, from Bodmin in Cornwall:

I have such an affinity with you. I feel your pain as if it were my own... When I wrote to you in 1984, you replied immediately because I was in the throes of a breakdown brought on by some of the same reasons that you yourself were brought down. The Catholic faith and my relationship with my Mother. I was at rock bottom, desperately ill when I wrote to you after reading *Our Kate*…

For the next few months you were my mother. You wrote many letters to me personally. My breakdown had caused agoraphobia but you created such love inside my barren mind for you, that I forced myself out of the house and made a long, terrifying journey on the bus and from then, into the library in search of your books. From that I was cured.

Catherine learned, at least as early as 1952 when she broadcast the piece on Woman's Hour called *Get Your Nerves Under Control*, that this was to be her purpose in life. Altruism may take a gigantic effort of self-absorption to achieve. A desire to share her 'brokenness with the world' may not have been the *reason* why she wrote the novels, but in writing them she became this 'giant, cosmic fountain from which all others could drink'. And, as we rake over the embers of her pyre, it is as well to remember it. Ultimately it did not bring her or Tom happiness, but perhaps the assumption that we are made to be happy is what holds many of us back.

Peace of mind was quite alien to Catherine. Her hate and aggression emanated from deep inside, but it was necessary to, and instrumental in, her purpose, and also, as Sarah herself is quick to point out, her sense of humour raised the status of her emotional repertoire to heroic levels at times.

Once she protested about typing up a character in *The Parson's Daughter*, who was too raw for her taste: 'I couldn't take the horrific parts she put in her books. There was one part when this character, the gentry bloke, who I hated, he took this girl down… and Catherine *knew* what I would think and said, "What do you think of him?" and I said, "He is terrible!" And she killed him off! Then she said, "What did you think of that?" I said I was delighted. And she said, 'Have you no compassion?' You had to laugh – I said, "Not a bit."'

But then, suddenly, something from outside would get confused and caught up with some complex element that so completely absorbed her psyche, and her aggression would pour onto the scene. People had begun to have to watch very carefully what they said in her company. 'I used to ring her every week' recalled Foster, 'and I had to write things down that I mustn't say, because if I let slip, bang! She'd be at me! She used to get inside you. She loved to have a hold over people, and if you ever went against anything then she could be threatening.' Foster then told me a story about a son of theirs, which is vintage Cookson material; anyone who knew her well would recognise Catherine's part in it immediately:

I've got ten grandchildren, she always used to send them money – birthdays, Christmas – except to my son Ross's children. Then one time in Jesmond she said to me, 'I'll never forgive Ross.' Now, years earlier Ross had jilted a girl. It wasn't an altar situation, he had a longterm relationship with a girl and he had packed her in. But she broke her heart, this girl. Catherine said, 'I know what it's like to feel jilted.' She was talking about this love affair when she was jilted [Jim Dailey]. So I just turned round and said, 'Aren't you pleased that you were jilted, otherwise you would never have met the marvellous man that you married?' And she went very quiet. And I came back to Hastings the following day and she actually apologised – I'd never known that before. She said she was sorry and she put a cheque in the post for £500 to Ross for the two children because she had never sent his children any money.'

What is characteristic in this story, besides Catherine's generosity, is that her formidable nature had always bowed to truth when it enlightened her perceptual framework. From within Catherine's narcissistic shell, Ross's jilting of his girlfriend *was* Jim Dailey's jilting of her fifty years earlier. At no point in the story did she change her mind about that. The change of heart came because Foster allowed her the indulgence of believing that, but guided her along a new line of consequences flowing *from* believing it. Had he said that likening Ross's action to Dailey's was preposterous, different circumstances, etc, he wouldn't have stood a chance.

The problem that people had with Catherine was not getting inside the shell but avoiding being caught on one of the negative hooks within it, and, once caught, making the fatal mistake of trying to shake free. She knew about these hooks and wrote about them in 1995 in *Plainer Still*, admitting that however hard she tried she couldn't help seeing the negative side of things. Foster had helped her along positive lines in this instance, and his grandchildren had reaped the reward.

Her formidable, self-orientated, testing, destructive but ultimately truthful nature made relationships into a tricky but potentially rewarding game of Diplomacy, in which there was the possibility of ambush or reward around every corner. For Cousin Sarah, who was the only family member other than Tom to be directly involved in the minutiae of Catherine's professional life, the potential for getting caught on a negative hook was far greater and almost ended in their estrangement.

On the professional level she met Catherine's expectations for seventeen years. The work rate was extraordinary, answering fan letters (Catherine received some 3,000 a year, all addresses were neatly filed), and typing some thirty-five manuscripts at least twice – the first draft plus one that followed Tom's editing; more when a mistake occasioned the re-typing of a page, for there were no word processors in those days and Tipex wasn't allowed because of the carbon copies required. Cousin Sarah has her own view as to what Mrs Thornton meant about Maggie Rowan riding to hell: 'The more I'd do, the more she'd give me to do, so it was impossible to please her.'

I worked with Catherine, too, and understand how professional she was, an absolute stickler. It was good training, but things could get fraught. 'When she was ill once, she was going into hospital and she asked me to look for a manuscript upstairs,' Sarah recalls. 'When she went into hospital all the work went in, you know, all the post. In Bristol Lodge in the cupboard I couldn't find this manuscript anywhere and I came down and she really went to town on me, and I came out of the bedroom and I started to cry, and Tom said, "Don't take any notice of her." I knew she was ill but she didn't have to be so nasty. Jack went to the hospital with the car to bring Tom back and Tom came back with a message from Kitty, "Tell Sarah I am sorry."'

'That was something. She never forgave. She never forgave Michael for what he said [about Kate being better than her] all those years ago. She never forgave anyone anything. Twice she apologised to me. That time from hospital, and before she died we had an up-and-downer and she rang me up and said, 'I would like to thank you for all the love you have given me over the years. Now that *was* an admission!'

In order to forgive, you have to be able to love. The blocks set up by the trauma of her birth were still in place, but she could get round them, often guided by Tom, and in her novels she got round them without help from anyone. That was her reward.

10 BECOMING KATE

Catherine returned to the North in 1976, and first took a house in Newcastle.

'It wasn't until they came up North to live that I really got to know Kitty,' Sarah told me. 'Some time beforehand she asked us to look round for a town house, we thought for when she came up to do talks and things. We found No 39 Eslington Terrace.'

Eslington Terrace is in Jesmond, a smart residential part of Newcastle. 'We sent the advert down for them to see and they came up to view the house. We thought it was just to be a holiday place, and it was for a while, we used to look after it when they weren't there.'

Catherine's move back to Newcastle in 1976 followed her move from publishers, Macdonalds, to William Heinemann for publication of *The Mallen Streak* in 1973. This was another turning point in Catherine's fortunes, occasioned four years earlier by literary agent Anthony Sheil taking over Christy & Moore, the agency that had represented Catherine from the start. The move from Macdonalds to Heinemann was the first step in Sheil's strategy for his new client, which was to step Catherine's career up a gear. Heinemann would give her front list exposure, there would be a TV adaptation of the novel, which would be followed by a 5-part BBC TV serial of her

179

childrens book, *Our John Willie,* set in a workhouse. *Katie Mulholland* would then be adapted into a musical, *The Fifteen Streets* into a play and a TV film watched by an audience of more than ten million viewers. The producer Ray Marshall would follow it up with a string of similar successes, and by then the pattern was long established whereby two books were published a year, each one moving effortlessly to the top of the bestseller list.

People tell me that Catherine moved North because she and Tom felt she wasn't getting the recognition she deserved in Hastings. Perhaps the granting of the Freedom of the Borough of South Shields in 1973 had got them thinking, but I believe it had much to do with the accelerating interest in the countryside, which led up to it, and Tom, in particular, seeing that their entrenchment in Northumbria would allow Catherine to root down not only imaginatively, but for real.

This idea of rooting down, of returning to the ground from which her people came, might seem to have made perfect sense to Catherine, whose whole life, post-breakdown, was bound up with the idea of rooting down in her mother culture, re-creating it, rooting her fictional characters in it. But did she actually need to be there? Recollection in the tranquillity of the sunken

Left: Catherine standing on the site of William Black Street after it had been levelled to the ground. Bottom left: Her greatest excitement on returning was taking the ferry from Shields to North Shields. Above: The Tyne Dock arches were torn down as she returned, sealing the area's history in the imaginative context of her earliest novels.

garden of Loreto had proved more than adequate. So the decision to leave Hastings was Tom's, perhaps guided by the feeling that a bit of real contact with the ground of her inspiration might be healthy.

While Catherine agreed to make the move, it proved a terrible wrench leaving Loreto. Foster recalls perfectly Catherine's mood after she handed over the keys and passed through the garden gate for the last time: 'I can still see her walking up the path, crying because she didn't want to leave here.' She had lived in Hastings for forty-seven years and had been happiest at Loreto, where her imagination had been given full rein: 'Once back in the North,' she told me, 'I was terribly homesick, not for Hastings or the South of England, but for Loreto, that lovely house and garden.'

I think it serves to confirm my thesis that as soon as they moved into the city bolt hole of 39 Eslington Terrace, they asked Sarah to look for something deeper in the countryside. 'I went round Ponteland way (north west of Newcastle), beyond there, towards Morpeth, and came upon a converted chapel at Kirkley. We told Catherine, they came to see it and bought it. It was lovely inside. Titled people had owned it and they were buried in the land.'

But Catherine and Tom never lived there. 'The man who was selling her the house said he knew who to take her to get a swimming pool put in,' Sarah remembers, 'and he introduced Catherine to John Anderson [a builder] at Town Barns, just out of Corbridge [west of Newcastle on the road to Hexham]. Now, Anderson's house was suddenly for sale. He had taken it off the market, but when Catherine arrived he put it back on... Anyway, it was a beautiful house, Town Barns, stone built with an indoor swimming pool, which is what she wanted. Trinity Barns is next door, she bought that, too, but never lived in it. She told someone that she had bought it for us, but we were never told about it. Then the girl who was in Trinity Barns had a cottage [further west] in Bardon Mill near Hadrian's Wall. It was an isolated cottage. They bought that too, and used it some weekends.'

It wasn't until I met Sarah that I realised just how Catherine and Tom had floundered around on their arrival in the North. In material terms it didn't matter that they bought all these properties because they could now afford to buy as many as they wanted, but it sapped their energy and took its toll on Catherine's health. Not long after they moved into Town Barns, she suffered a series of heart attacks, two more serious than the others, but all requiring hospital treatment.

On arrival in Corbridge they had registered as private patients with Dr David Harle, and Catherine soon realised that she had at last found someone she could respect and depend upon in the medical department. He brooked no dissent in his patients and Catherine found herself bending to his carefully orchestrated will with an unusual degree of compliance. For his part he admired the fortitude of a woman who had suffered numerous ailments over the years, 'any one of which would have been enough for most of us to cope with,' but was less enamoured of her bad temper and knack of seeing the worst in people. Nevertheless, he became her close confidant and true friend, which fact Catherine treasured.

Town Barns itself was less successful. Back in the bosom of her people for real, was, Catherine discovered, more fraught with difficulty than finding her place in it in imagination. Part of the land attached to the properties had been granted planning permission for dwellings. Tom turned it into a garden, beautifully landscaped and planted from scratch. Unaccountably, this put local noses out of joint: incomers moving in, depriving the natives of housing, contravening preservation guidelines, flaunting their wealth, etc, etc. And when Catherine's illness kept her out of the public eye, they complained that she was stand-offish. Soon Catherine and Tom began receiving anonymous letters and at least one abusive telephone call. Then Tom spotted someone shooting movie film of them through the bedroom window, 'but the climax came,' Catherine told me, 'when Tom was stopped in the street one day by a beaming lady who told him gleefully that she had put me on a rota of the sightseeing bus in Durham. During the vac they let students' rooms to different companies and the town provided a bus for sightseeing. Twice before this we'd had a bus full of people unload at the gate, and it wasn't a very big front garden and it wasn't a very big yard leading to the garage, so they were almost on top of us and we

The Tyne snakes past Tyne Dock and Shields to the North Sea after the demolition of the New Buildings and the Slake, now much of it a car park. Tyne Dock is still in place, and at the bottom right

corner of the picture, the site of the New Buildings estate can be seen, now a light industrial park, beyond which, out of picture, lies a garage, the site of No 5 Leam Lane, where Catherine was born.

just had to get away.' Then, in January 1981, they were burgled.

The total experience of coming North did, however, succeed in one way in that it took them ever further west out of the city, ever deeper into the countryside she loved, and it was while they were looking for a setting for *A Dinner of Herbs* that they came upon the village of Langley and 'our bungalow

up in the hills.' Langley grew up in the 18th century around a mill used for smelting lead ore, mined on Alston Moor. The stunning lake, which met the garden of the bungalow called Bristol Lodge was originally dammed to supply water to a smelting works in nearby woodland, which, with the disused lead ore railway and a 30m-high chimney connected to the old mill by means of a mile-long, underground flue, all attest to the industry on which villagers once subsisted.

Finally, they had found a place that met all their requirements. They had found what they had come North for.

Bristol Lodge was already more than a bungalow when they arrived: 'Attached to it was a 200-year-old cottage. We gutted the old cottage and made it into a nice apartment. We built upwards on top of the flat roof and made a 40-foot study and we turned an awful, dirty swimming pool that was attached to the conservatory into a 50-foot drawing room and above that made a 40-foot bedroom *en suite,* which was really a beautiful piece. Tom took over the garden as always and I over the house, and there we were.'

Some of Catherine's best late novels take from the spirit of this place. For example, she brings the landscape alive in the main character in *A Dinner*

Left: Langley, Northumberland, seven miles from Hexham and between Haydon Bridge and Allendale Town. The village, right, grew up around a lead smelting works in the 18th century. In the trees opposite can be found relics of the industry, a railway embankment and mine shaft opening.

of Herbs, the strange, witch-like herbalist, Kate Makepeace, and Bristol Lodge stands on the banks of the lake which is the moonlit setting of Robert Bradley's first meeting with Millie in *The Moth*, the goddess figure who leads Robert to his destiny.

Catherine had set earlier novels in the area, like *The Dwelling Place*, *Feathers in the Fire*, the *Mallen* trilogy and *The Girl*, but only now that she was part of it could she create character as mature as Makepeace, a woman who is the true personification of the land in which she dwells. Kate Makepeace emerges from the shadows, a Mother Earth figure, touchstone of everyone's lives, strange, magical, a spirit substance, and, as again with Millie in *The Moth*, we have the connection between an intuitional woman and the moon. Kate is seen as the moon, skipping over the waves at night, but never less than real.

Kate is a wizard with her herbs, a healer, like Catherine is to the characters of her fiction, resolving their fears. People derive their strength from her. In Kate Makepeace, Catherine, the actress, does indeed *become* the part. She is the mythic figure with which she had originally identified her mother in *Kate Hannigan*. Hers had of course always been a search within her own self, even when Kate was intermediary.

As the identification between mother and daughter is made explicit in the novel, Kate Makepeace dies and is returned to the ground from which she emerged.

This is Catherine fulfilling the ultimate purpose of her coming home, to die among her own folk, but it is also Catherine establishing Mother Earth as both giver of life and taker, the womb as cold as a tomb, which is reminiscent

of Emily Bronte – there was nothing sweet about Catherine Cookson either, but plenty that was true.

In 1985 she received the OBE from the Queen. There followed her eightieth birthday, from which she seemed to gain a certain immortality, the press beginning to refer to her as an Icon of the North. In the same year there was a second move of publisher to the even more high profile Bantam Press, the parent company of the imprint Corgi Books, which had published her in paperback for nearly thirty years. Seven years later she was made a Dame of the British Empire. Five years after that, in June 1998, she died.

In private, there was anything but a peaceful passage to the end. If *Dinner of Herbs* had spelled out the truth to which she had been journeying, it did little to assuage her troubled mind. 'There were bouts of black depression,' remembers Sarah. It was while they were living at Bristol Lodge that Tom threatened divorce. There were, however, also see-sawing moments of near religious ecstasy as she turned over and over in her mind what she did or did not believe about God and the after-life. One followed a television programme which showed the face of Christ portrayed on the great stained-glass window of Buckfast Abbey in Devon. It filled the screen and in an instant – 'swifter than an atom of a second,' as she put it – Catherine was enveloped in a feeling of unbelievable peace. 'I was enveloped in it. It filled every pore of my life. In all my life I had never experienced anything like it. I turned my head and saw Tom standing at the drawing room door, his face was alight and what he said astounded me even more, "Oh," he cried, "I felt it!" Then he came to me and held me.'

That was Tom.

Catherine had her publisher send to Buckfast Abbey for photographs of the stained glass window, and they slept with these cards under their pillows until they died.

During this period a Roman Catholic priest by name of Tom Power became a close friend of Catherine and twice wrote to the Pope about her so that, as Catherine told me, he 'signed plaques, one for my 80th birthday and one for my 90th. Dear soul, he still thinks God will have a place for me in his Kingdom.' But Father Power would find out the hard way that while Catherine could accept a spiritual dimension and hold it true, anything that smacked of the Church as institution she could not stomach. 'Father Tom Power had tried for years to win me over to the faith until he realised that he was flogging a dead horse. But he maintained that I was more with God and more religious than anyone he knew of. Well, I told him [about her experience with the stained-glass image of Christ]. Was he ecstatic? He said he knew that God

The stunning lake (left), which met the garden of a bungalow called Bristol Lodge, was originally dammed to supply water to the smelting works. Finally, in 1981, they had found a place that met all their requirements. They had found what they had come north for.

Below right: the back of the Lodge. 'Like all the houses we had, I must change and arrange and we built upwards and side-wards and made a 200 year old cottage into a beautiful apartment. It was a wonderful place.'

The garden, as always, was Tom's province.

would work his way in the end. He left the house quickly, went to his little church in Haydon Bridge and what did he carry back? The almost life-size statue of Our Lady, a bag filled with rosaries, crosses, medallions, holy water, everything, all the things I had been fighting against all my thinking life, all these things that were held up with intermediaries to God. He had left them at the front door. When Tom brought them in I yelled at him, "Get them away! Get them away!" Even the sight of them was shattering my peace....'

You could say that this was outrageous behaviour on Catherine's part, or that Father Power should have known better. It was a sign that the battle within herself was not quite over, perhaps that she knew her desire to be her own woman, integrated, independent of the myths most of us need to live by, would never be fulfilled.

The paraphernalia of Catholicism was anathema to her because it reminded her that she had not come as far as she would have liked, otherwise why was she sleeping with a postcard of Buckfast Abbey under her pillow? So confused had she become in the last decades of her life about religion that when Sister Catherine came to England with a group of black kids from Los Angeles, who knew Catherine through her novels, which the nun had read to them, she refused to receive them. The presence of a Roman Catholic nun in the house troubled her too deeply. Fortunately, the damage to what was so important a relationship was later repaired. As the end approached she began to accept the limits of her struggle for independence, telling me in 1996 that when Father Power 'visits me now, he asks if he can say a prayer of peace over me and this he does. And you know, strangely, when he lays his hand on my brow I have a momentary feeling of the night of Buckfast Abbey.'

The chapel in St Peter & Paul's Tyne Dock, where Catherine knelt as a child. She would be reconciled to her faith before she died.

The five heart attacks in 1977/8 were followed by two in 1990, and, in between, there were 30-mile, emergency flights from Bristol Lodge to hospital in Newcastle due to the telangiectasic bleeding, if a wound could not be plugged or cauterised at home. In the end, this led to her Consultant, Hugo Marshall, insisting that she move closer to the city. His wife, Ann, also a doctor, found White Lodge in Jesmond, just a stone's throw from Eslington Terrace. Catherine and Tom moved there in 1991.

Five years later, Catherine told me that she had been out of the house on three occasions only – 'special events' – other than to go to the hospital. Most of the time she lay in bed in a downstairs room, looking out onto the garden, as Kate had. In 1994 Sarah herself suffered a heart attack. By then Ann had become Catherine's companion, quietly organising her work and keeping the world at bay, ably assisted by Catherine's housekeeper, Noreen White.

By 1997 Catherine was having transfusions of two pints of blood every two or three weeks, dismissing the problem to me by saying, 'But I've still got one ace up my sleeve, and that's my WP [her will power], so we'll only have to wait and see who wins.'

At that point she was writing *The Silent Lady*, which she assured me was her best novel to date, until her editor at Bantam, the late Alan Earney, told her

Catherine and Tom pictured beside the lake at Bristol Lodge, where they lived for ten years, before the trips to hospital in Newcastle became so frequent that they were forced back into the city.

it was not and she shared the news with me with a nod to his better judgement. She never lost her sense of humour.

It was characteristic of the people to whom I spoke in researching *Kate's Daughter* that they were pleased at last to have the opportunity to say what they really felt about Catherine, which was that she could be very hurtful and demanding and bitter. She was these things and she was also generous – her gifts to educational and medical institutions I have barely touched on – encouraging, and a champion of effort and truth.

She was, as Mannie Anderson diagnosed, a cyclic personality – she swayed one way and then the other, from being creative to being destructive. But none of us is completely in touch with our creative (unifying, loving) side – our *Eros* – in complete defiance of our *Thanaton*, and if we were we would have opted out of life.

I have attempted to show how and why Catherine became obsessed with her destructive side, which became malignant, and that she was a victim in this, and how the novels were a channel to drain the malignance out of her, but served to return her to the source of it, and how Tom tried to create an environment in which she might nurture her creative, unifying, loving side, from which she had become part separated even before the chimney-piece episode, indeed, I have suggested, even before she was born.

Through the final years, Tom never faltered. The last time I visited the house he was beside the bed holding her hand through the hour that I stayed. This was his elected position until the end. Ultimately, since their meeting in 1936, there was only the two of them – 'thee and me,' as Catherine put it in a poem in *Plainer Still*.

Then, in the Spring of 1998, her life was brought full circle. 'For all the doubts about her faith over the years,' said Cousin Sarah, 'she asked me to contact a priest from St Peter & Paul, Tyne Dock. Father Ian Jackson called to see her and she was reconciled to the Catholic Church.' A few months later, on Thursday June 11, in the ground floor bedroom where she had passed the last years of her life, the roses tapping at the window from the flower bed outside, she died. Twelve days later, Tom was admitted to hospital and died on the following Sunday.

Sister Catherine's judgement that her namesake's contribution was to share her 'brokenness' with the world, is compelling. To reach us, Catherine needed her aloneness, her separateness and the traumatic experience of childhood. Without her psychic crippledness, where would the bridges she built into our safer world have come from?

In that sense, Catherine was her art, more even than the novels.

Right: View over her beloved Shap Fell, at dusk.

ACKNOWLEDGMENTS

In particular I would like to thank Sarah Sables, Catherine's cousin, confidante and sometime PA, for her unstinting encouragement and co-operation in the writing of this book, and for many of the family photographs that appear in it.

I am also deeply indebted to Boston University for permission to use hitherto unpublished material (text and photographs) in The Catherine Cookson Collection in Special Collections at the University, and to Bantam Press, publishers of Catherine's novels and non-fiction, a complete list of which is available on page 2. Acknowledgment is also made to *A Child of the Tyne: Autobiographies* by James Kirkup, published by Poetry Salzburg (formerly the University of Salzburg Press), *Francie* by Frances Nichols, published by Tups Books, Newcastle, *The Anatomy of Human Destructiveness* by Erich Fromm, published by Pimlico, an imprint of Random House, and *The Christian Agnostic by* Leslie D Weatherhead, published by Hodder Headline.

Many thanks, too, for their generous co-operation in interview and sometimes in giving photographs, to Catherine and Tom's relations: Rosemary and Foster Barker, Theresa Neville, Edna Humphreys, and close friend Dr Mannie Anderson, also friends and acquaintances from childhood and later, Winnie Richardson, Reny Harding, John Atkinson, Joan Moules, Tony Weeks-Pearson, James Davidson, Steve Blower and John Finch, and my thanks to Hugo and Ann Marshall for their quiet encouragement, to Doris Johnson, whose incisive analysis was very much appreciated, to Tyne Tees Television, Granada Television, *The Sunday Telegraph Magazine* and to The Harry Edwards Spiritual Healing Sanctuary.

The *Shields Gazette*, Britain's oldest evening newspaper, was instrumental in turning up a number of important leads – my gratitude to them for this and for permission to use text and photographs of Catherine and the local area, also to Keith Bardwell and the Local History section of the South Shields Library, and to Hastings Library, the Hastings Museum and the Newcastle Discovery Museum for access to their written records and for permission to use photographs. Similarly, I would like to thank Vince Rea of the Bede Gallery (Jarrow), the owners of the Gibson Photographic Collection and the Northumberland Record Office, Festival Film & TV Ltd, Peter Higginbotham, Rosemary and Foster Barker, and the Newcastle City Library for permission to use photographs from their collections.

Every effort has been made to trace copyright owners, and I would be grateful to hear from any that I may have failed to acknowledge.